The Centers of Civilization Series

LONDON

in the Age of Chaucer

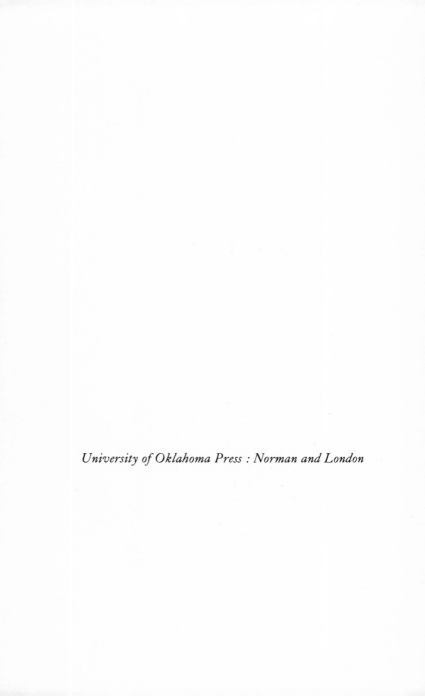

University of Oklahoma Press : Norman and London

LONDON

in the Age of Chaucer

by A. R. Myers

Library of Congress Catalog Card Number: 73 – 177342
ISBN: 0 – 8061 – 0997 – 1
ISBN: 0 – 8061 – 2111 – 4 (pbk.)

London in the Age of Chaucer is Volume 31 in *The Centers of Civilization Series*.

For Rosalind and Christabel

Acknowledgments

I should like to thank Professor C. N. L. Brooke for his generous help both in reading the manuscript of this book despite his own heavy work commitments and in making valuable suggestions. I should also like to thank my daughters, Rosalind and Christabel, who read the manuscript and applied to it a very useful combination of historical training and common sense. For any remaining errors and defects I am entirely responsible.

West Kirby
Cheshire
England

A. R. MYERS

Contents

MAP

LONDON

in the Age of Chaucer

II

The Face of London

If a modern observer could suddenly be transported back
to the London of Chaucer, his first impression would
probably be of a busy but small market town. He would
be struck by the stalls laden with country produce in the
main streets, the country folk crying their wares, the
trees and gardens within the walls, the pigs and poultry in
the streets, the farmyard smells, and the nearness of the
countryside. For the area of London within its walls was
less than a square mile; from east to west it had spread,
with the attraction of river transport, for about a mile, but
from south to north it had grown to little more than 1,000
yards at the widest point. It is true that the population had
overflowed into suburbs beyond the walls, but as yet these
faubourgs were small and for the most part sparsely
peopled.

The largest suburb was the one on the west. In the late
twelfth century William FitzStephen, Thomas Becket's
biographer, had described it as "a populous suburb." But
his account of London is so incredibly eulogistic that one

3

has to take most of his judgments with a large pinch of salt. There is reason to believe that this western suburb had increased much in importance since FitzStephen's time; in 1394 a new ward was created, that of Farringdon Without (the walls), divided from Farringdon Within. This new ward, entered from the walled city at Ludgate, ended on Fleet Street at Temple Bar, where there was a bar across the road to mark the extent of the City of London's jurisdiction.

By Chaucer's day bishops' inns stretched almost continuously along the south side of the Strand from Temple Bar to Charing Cross. The most important exceptions were the Savoy Palace of John of Gaunt and the site of the present Charing Cross Railway Station, on which the Hungerford family built a house in the early fifteenth century. On the north side of the Strand houses had been built from London to the west end of Holywell, near the present church of St. Mary-le-Strand, but the development on this side was mere ribbon building. Until the reign of Elizabeth I the whole area behind the houses on the west side of Chancery Lane and the north side of the Strand, all the way to the hamlet around St. Giles-in-the-Fields, with its leper hospital, remained open fields. Where the Law Courts were to be erected in late Victorian days were Fickets Fields, a spot so lonely at night that the Lollards could hope to make it their undetected rendezvous for their attempted rising in 1414.

The way via the Strand to Westminster led through the small but fashionable village of Charing. There, on the site of the present Trafalgar Square, stood the Royal

Mews. Nearby, in 1294, Edward I had erected the last of his memorial crosses to his beloved Queen Eleanor. At this point the main road swung to the right, to lead through the fields to Knightsbridge and the west; but a muddy side road on the left led to Westminster, the road that was later to be famous as Whitehall. In Chaucer's day, on the right side of the road, on the site of the present Admiralty, Horse Guards and other government offices, backed by St. James's Park, lay fields and gardens mostly belonging to the abbot and convent of Westminster. On the left side at Charing Cross the traveler would pass the Augustinian House of St. Mary, which belonged to Roncesvalles, or Roncevaux, in the Pyrenees. Chaucer's iniquitous Pardoner was said to be "of Rounceval," for this house had a reputation of making money by selling pardons. The French wars had stirred up anti-French feeling, and in 1379 the king seized the buildings and extensive grounds of this house. After St. Mary Rounceval the traveler to Westminster passed the even larger area, stretching down to the river and as yet largely without buildings, called "Scotland"—named not for the king of Scots, as was later surmised, but for one Adam Scot, who had owned it in Edward I's day. Next to Scotland was York Place, the impressive inn of the archbishops of York, whose great gardens also stretched down to the Thames. So desirable was York Place that, on the downfall of Cardinal Thomas Wolsey, Archbishop of York, it aroused the cupidity of Henry VIII, who seized it and turned it into the nucleus of the great Whitehall Palace.

In Chaucer's day the road narrowed at York Place and,

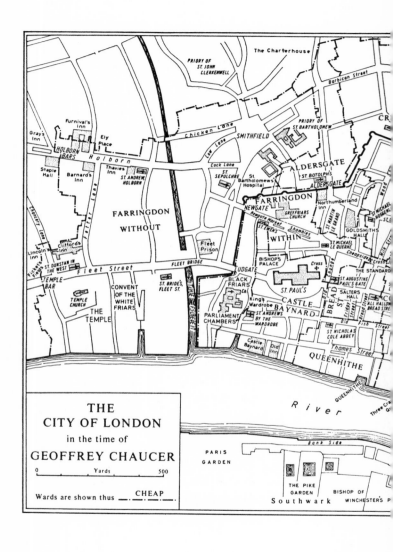

THE
CITY OF LONDON
in the time of

GEOFFREY CHAUCER

0   Yards   500

Wards are shown thus ___.___.___.   CHEAP

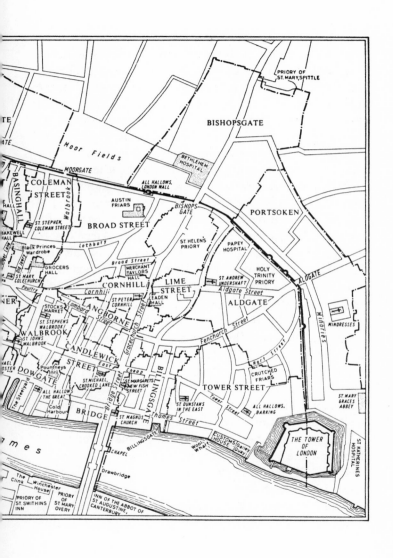

as King Street, led into the village of Westminster. To accommodate some of the many visitors who came to the abbey and the palace of Westminster, inns had already been established, some of them to become famous, like the Bell, in King Street, and the Cock and Tabard, in Tothill Street. To cater for the needs of these visitors and of the resident governing classes of monks, courtiers, and government officials, a population of several hundred tradesmen, craftsmen, servants, and porters had gathered there. At Westminster, however, there were in addition two groups, not easily distinguishable from one another, of less desirable residents. The indiscriminate charity of a wealthy abbey, so near to the comparatively large city of London, attracted not only the deserving poor but also the shiftless. And Westminster Abbey, with its extensive privileges of sanctuary for fugitives from justice or vengeance, unwittingly encouraged not only meritorious refugees but also thieves, pimps, murderers, and other criminals, who made the sanctuary a base for their activities. From the days of Chaucer's boyhood the narrow road of mean houses just northwest of the sanctuary of the abbey was known as Thieves' Lane, from the dominant occupation of its inhabitants. There were other streets in Westminster occupied by criminals and feckless poor.

The government of this large village was shared by the abbot and the royal officials, who co-operated rather ineffectively. Their inadequate attempts to preserve law and order did not, however, prevent peaceful activities, which must have impressed the visitor to Westminster. South of the abbey, on the marshy but fertile soil of Tothill Fields, were some of the abbey's orchards and gardens, producing luxuries like asparagus and figs and supplementing the food the abbey drew from its convent, or Covent, Garden on the east. In the abbey precinct were luxury trades catering to the monks and the courtiers; it was no accident that Caxton later established his printing press there. From 1389 to 1391 Chaucer was clerk of the king's works at Westminster. While serving in this capacity he must have seen much of the bustle of masons and carpenters and the delivery of stone and timber to the abbey for the building of the nave (largely on the initiative of Richard II) in the style that Henry III had used for the east end over one hundred years before. When he went back to Westminster in the late 1390's, Chaucer would see the carpenters reroofing Westminster Hall with the glorious hammer-beam roof, almost seventy feet in span, designed by Hugh Herland. The closeness of the relations between the Crown and the abbey is illustrated by Chaucer's last residence. In December, 1399, the government provided him with a "tenement" in the garden of the Lady Chapel of Westminster Abbey.

The development of Westminster, so intimately linked with that of London, had no parallel in London's neighborhood. Westminster's only rival in population was Southwark, which, unlike Westminster, owed its existence to its great neighbor. Until the opening of Westminster Bridge in 1750, London Bridge was the only road crossing the Thames in its lower reaches. The many travelers to London from the south had to pass through Southwark. There they might find it convenient to stay the night before entering the city by water or by the bridge. Hence a number of inns had been established in Southwark, and these, like Chaucer's Tabard Inn, formed convenient places of assembly for parties setting off for Canterbury or the Continent.

The traveler to or from London through Southwark would not have found all the buildings or inhabitants of Southwark as respectable as the Tabard Inn and its host. It is true that some great persons who went to London from south of the Thames, such as the Bishop of Winchester or the Abbot of St. Augustine's Canterbury, found it convenient to have houses in Southwark rather than to try to accommodate their large households in the city itself. Below this social level were inhabitants of Southwark whose means of livelihood the traveler would have found both respectable and pleasing. Such were the cattle herders who might have been seen by men from Kent, driving their cattle up the Old Kent Road, or the market gardeners working in the fields between Southwark and the priory of Bermondsey. (The Bishop of Winchester's manor kept a large number of swine and grew much fruit, especially apples.) The herders and gardeners produced food for the London market.

Southwark also had a growing number of respectable but unpleasant activities. London needed industries which it was disagreeable to have too close. Thus in Southwark a tannery was in operation and kilns were in use for smelting and lime burning (smoke from the newfangled coal was arousing protests from the great lords in Southwark).

Southwark also had many residents who lived there

because of its comparative lawlessness. In 1327 a charter of Edward III gave the city financial control but imperfect authority to maintain order, for which in theory the sheriff of Surrey was still partly responsible. Hence craftsmen who did not wish, or were not allowed, to join a city guild and did not choose to go to Westminster found refuge in Southwark and took the risk of selling their goods illegally in London. Prostitutes, driven out of London by the prudish outlook of the city fathers, congregated in Southwark, where they would be unmolested and to which their clients would easily be able to come for a pleasant evening trip from London. There were indeed so many bawdyhouses—often inns, baths, and brothels all in one—in the liberty of the Bishop of Winchester, along the river front at Bankside (in spite of his riverside prison, the Clink), that in London whores were often known as "Winchester geese." These dubious taverns were also haunts of cutthroats and pickpockets, who found the greater laxity of Southwark's government (like that of Westminster) more to their liking than the stricter surveillance of London. Moreover, the Southwark waterfront was very handy for an attempt at burglary in London by boat on a dark night. So Southwark was well known not only for its great houses and its many inns but also for its harlots and its criminals. But again, by modern standards it was very small and probably had little more than a thousand inhabitants. A few hundred yards from the bridge, where the High Street divided into the Newington and Dover roads, the houses thinned out and gave way to fields.

Apart from Westminster and Southwark there were no considerable townships in the London area outside the City's jurisdiction, and in Chaucer's day any able-bodied Londoner could walk out of it into open countryside within half an hour. London was not only small by modern standards but smaller than several contemporary cities in Europe. In 1377, London's population was, according to the poll-tax returns of that year, about forty thousand. It had fewer inhabitants than Milan, Venice, Florence, Naples, Ghent, and Paris and was about the size of Bruges, Louvain, Brussels, Ypres, Barcelona, Seville, Cordova, Granada, Cologne, and Lübeck.

Apart from the roads to Westminster and Southwark there was none of the suburban sprawl that developed in the seventeenth century, and the open country began almost at once on all the other roads out of London. For example, on Holborn, the other great westerly route out of London, there was very little building in Chaucer's day beyond Holborn Bars. Just outside the bars on the south side a rich mercer had erected Staple Hall, a pillared, or "stapled," hall, one of the very few half-timbered houses of London still preserved today. Next to Staple Inn was the Old Temple, which had been the London house of the Bishop of Lincoln since the twelfth century. Beyond the Old Temple was the Bishop of Chichester's Inn, near the top of Chancery Lane. But here the building seems to have stopped, and the traveler westward would, if he had time to lift his eyes from the puddles of the muddy lanes, have seen St. Giles's Church in the distance, among the trees and fields. On the north side of Holborn the only edifice of importance outside the bars was a great house, or inn, standing in a large garden. It belonged to Lord Gray of Wilton, who in 1397 leased it to the lawyers to become an Inn of Court.

On the north side of the city the ward of Farringdon Without extended only a few yards beyond Smithfield, a green space surrounded by trees, where a horse fair and cattle market took place on Saturdays and tournaments and games were held. Outside the bars on this side were only a few great ecclesiastical foundations. Ely Place, the London house of the bishops of Ely, had just been rebuilt by Thomas Arundel. It had a very large garden, to become famous in Shakespeare's day for its strawberries and producing in Chaucer's day enough vegetables to sell some at a profit. On the east, across Holborn Stream (which below Holborn Bridge was tidal and was called the Fleet River), a few dwellings were beginning to cluster round four monastic houses. The Priory of St. John Clerkenwell was the headquarters in England of the knightly order of St. John of Jerusalem. The buildings were burned down by the rebels of 1381, who did not allow anyone to quench the fires for several days. In Chaucer's later years the prior was busy rebuilding both church and priory. North of St. John's lay the much poorer Augustinian nunnery of St. Mary's Clerkenwell, almost surrounded by fields. Next to St. John's on the southeast was the Charterhouse, founded in 1371 by one of Edward III's famous captains, Sir Walter de Manny, so that the revered Carthusian monks might pray in perpetuity for his soul and the souls of his wife and friends,

as well as for the great number of plague victims buried
there. In 1349 he had out of pity bought thirteen acres of
ground there, away from human habitation to provide a
burial site for plague victims without spreading the dread
disease, as burial in a city churchyard might do. South of
the Charterhouse lay another of the great religious houses
which were so conspicuous a feature of London before the
Reformation. This was the great Priory of St. Bartholomew, with its splendid Norman and Early English
church and its churchyard, in which for three days every
year at St. Bartholomewtide (August 24) a cloth fair was
held for the clothiers of all England. Southwest of the
great priory lay St. Bartholomew's Hospital, founded in
the twelfth century and already famous for its care of the
poor and diseased.

East of St. Bartholomew's and the Charterhouse lay
the wards of Aldersgate and Cripplegate, whose names
recalled the gates in the walls, just as the Barbican paid
testimony to the outwork beyond. East of Cripplegate the
marshes of Moor Fields came right up to the city walls.
In early Roman times the marsh had not existed. The
building of the wall had obstructed the little river, the
Walbrook, which flowed that way to the Thames. The
ground there had turned into the swamp it was to remain
until the sixteenth century. Londoners skated on the
marshes in winter and on fine summer evenings took walks
there before the ringing of the curfew warned them that
the city gates were about to shut for the night. In the year
of Agincourt, 1415, the mayor was to make a postern called
Moorgate, to enable the citizens to reach the fens more

quickly and walk, on causeways through them, to the villages of Islington and Hoxton. The new gate was also meant to make it easier for youths to practice archery there, for national defense—though in fact it seems to have made it easier for them to play forbidden games like football and hockey as well.

To the east of Moor Fields the wards of Bishopsgate and Portsoken lay outside the walls. Just beyond Bishopsgate was Bethlehem, or Bedlam, Hospital, already noted for its care of lunatics. Farther out, on the right of the road, was the priory of St. Mary Spittle, which had at the Dissolution, according to Stow, 180 beds for poor persons. (It is a useful corrective to the old notion that it was the Puritans who started a love of sermons if we reflect that already in Chaucer's day it was a custom for Londoners to go out on Easter Monday, Tuesday, and Wednesday, to Spittle Pulpit Cross, to hear Easter sermons. The mayor and aldermen attended on these occasions; perhaps they were encouraged to do so by being able to wear scarlet liveries on Easter Monday and Tuesday and violet on Wednesday.)

Along the road beyond Bishopsgate the houses lined the street for some distance, but behind them was open country. Portsoken ward, farther south, was already more thickly settled, but there was still a great deal of open ground there, some of it used as tenteryards for stretching cloth. The entrance through the wall on the east side of the city was at Aldgate, and above this gate Chaucer lived in a dwelling which he rented from the city authorities for twelve years, from 1374 to 1386. From this dwelling he could have witnessed some stirring events, such as the provision of a portcullis and chains at the gate in 1377, when there was a scare of French invasion, and the breaking into the city during the night by the rebels in June, 1381, through this gate, owing to the connivance of Alderman William Tonge. Even in peaceful times there was much to see from Chaucer's room over Aldgate, for tolls for the repair of the road were exacted at the gate. The tariff shows the predominantly rural character of the incoming traffic: iron-bound carts bringing food paid twopence, carts not iron bound bringing dung were charged a penny, and horses laden with grain had to contribute a halfpenny. From his window over Aldgate Chaucer could have seen, besides all this busy traffic and the pedestrians mingling with it, the rutted road winding away toward Whitechapel in the fields and, farther away, to Bethnal Green and Stepney, where London merchants were beginning to put up pleasant country houses. It is true that the ward of Portsoken, lying just outside the wall to the east of Aldgate, was filling up with a mainly laboring population who worked for the cannon makers, the bell founders, the glaziers, and other workshops of the Aldgate area. But on this side of London, too, Chaucer could quickly have been out among the fields and meadows. So rural was the area beyond Portsoken that, in 1325, the Dean of St. Paul's sent out some of his servants to guard his crops at Stepney during the night.

But Londoners did not need to leave the city to see trees and gardens or to be reminded of country ways. A great number of the houses in the city had back gardens where the householder might grow herbs, draw his water from a well, and stroll for recreation. Gardeners sold their produce in front of the church of St. Augustine at the east gate of St. Paul's churchyard until 1345. They made so much noise crying their wares that the services inside the church were disturbed and they had to remove to the space between the south gate of the churchyard and the garden wall of the Blackfriars. The northwest approaches to Smithfield were evocative of the traffic along them to Smithfield Market and to the city beyond—Cowcross Street, Chicken Lane, Cow Lane, Cock Lane. Once bought for meat, cattle were taken only a few hundred yards farther south to Newgate, where the names of Butchers' Row and the Shambles remind us of what went on there. The hens were mostly taken on to the east end of Cheapside, where they were sold at the Poultry, which was also a market for fish. Customers were served from stalls placed in the middle of what was the chief street of London and which still had many of the features of a country market. At the west end of this road, Newgate was congested with butchers' stalls, which were becoming permanent and dividing the road into two narrow lanes. There had been trouble over this as long ago as 1273, when the mayor had ordered the stalls to be removed for the passage of Edward I, expected back from the Holy Land. The stallholders were angry, for all of them paid rent and some had a life tenancy. The City authorities tried to conciliate them by founding a new market for fish and flesh to the east of the Poultry in 1282; but the Newgate traders stuck to their old site, and the result was that London got two meat markets in the one main street.

This new market was sited where there had long been a pair of stocks and where the Mansion House now stands. In order to help the upkeep of London Bridge by the income from this market, the city government tried hard to make the Stocks Market the only legal selling spot for fish in London and the most important one for meat. Traders who tried to sell fish elsewhere were had up in court; if they persisted, London citizens were deprived of the freedom of the City and non-Londoners or "foreigners" were fined. The latter were specially tempted to sell in back streets, because there was much competition and surveillance in the Stocks Market and because there they were not allowed to take home any fish at the end of the day. If they had any left over, it therefore had to be sold cheap. Yet in spite of these surreptitious sales of fish elsewhere (especially Old Fish Street), the Stocks Market presented as animated a scene in Chaucer's day as the Poultry and Newgate markets.

The busy traveler from Holborn who had struggled past all these stalls and their importuning and shouting stallholders had further obstacles to encounter before he reached Aldgate along this main street. To the east of the Stocks Market there was a corn market in Cornhill (with another corn market in Gracechurch Street), and beyond Cornhill yet another meat (including poultry) market at Leadenhall Market, with more butchers' stalls cluttering the street and more entrails lying about to offend the nose

and impede one's progress by the number of stray dogs
and cats and pigs that they attracted. If our traveler had
glanced down some of the narrow lanes that he passed,
many of them only six to nine feet wide with overhanging
houses that nearly met, he would have seen further street
trading in country products—Gutter, or Gutheron's,
Lane, where bread from Stratford-le-Bow was sold from
the carts that brought it to London, Bread Street, Milk
Street, and Honey Lane. The impression of a market town
would have been enhanced by the number of pigs roaming
about the streets, snuffling for food among the rubbish
from the stalls and houses and sometimes making trouble.
In 1332 we read of a sow that strayed through the open
door of a shop and bit a month-old baby lying in its cradle,
causing its death.

Street hawkers cried their country wares, from laven-
der to apples, adding to the din. There seem to have been
trees within the walls, not only in gardens but on common
ground. In 1314 the men of Broad Street ward asked the
mayor and aldermen if an old elm growing by London
Wall near Bishopsgate might be cut down and sold, the
proceeds to be used to buy a hook with chains and cords
for their ward. This would be used, as usual, for throwing
on to the roof of a burning wooden house, to pull down
the house and stop the flames from spreading. The
countryside was so near that rushes were commonly used
as floor coverings and great quantities were brought into
the city. Indeed, special regulations had to be made to
ensure that the streets were not littered with them when
they were carried from the barges and carts.

But though London had these and other signs of a market town, it was already much more than that. It was also a great commercial center and the wealthiest and most populous town in England. These features were reflected in its appearance. To take the population first, the poll-tax returns of 1377 are not easy to interpret, but they are much the best figures that we have for this period; though the absolute figures may be wrong, the ratios between towns are likely to be fairly accurate. In contrast to London's population of about 40,000, the next two towns in size, York and Bristol, were only about 10,000, followed by Coventry with about 7,000, Norwich with 6,000, and Lincoln with 5,000. In size, therefore, London was in a class by itself, and to Englishmen from other towns it looked enormous. The contrast was not only in size but also in wealth, for more and more of the trade of the realm was centering on the city.

Since the thirteenth century London had become increasingly dominant in the declining but still important trade in the export of wool. In the reign of Edward I (1272–1307), Boston had been the chief port for this; by the reign of Richard II (1377–99) London was pre-eminent. By this time London merchants were the leaders of the Company of the Staple which controlled wool as far away as the Cotswolds. Already by the date of Chaucer's birth (c. 1340) over 40 per cent of the total exports of English wool were going out through London, and by the time he died (1400) the London share was well over half. To London's predominance in wool export was being added a growing importance in the rapidly increasing ex-

port trade in cloth, the commodity which in the early
fifteenth century was to become England's most important
export. In so far as cloth was not handled by aliens, like
the Italians or the Hansard merchants of Germany, it was
exported by the Merchant Adventurers, of whom the
majority and the most wealthy were Londoners. London
had an advantage over the traders of most other leading
English ports, such as Newcastle, Hull, Boston, or Bristol,
in that it was so well situated for the trade with the Netherlands, which, except for Italy, supplied the chief market
both for English wool and English cloth. To the discontent of provincial merchants, Londoners not only dominated the Company of the Staple but were pre-eminent
among the Merchant Adventurers who traded in the
Netherlands. The career of William Caxton was to show
that this could bring a London Merchant Adventurer into
close contact with the highest circles both in the Netherlands and in England.

But London was not dependent solely on the wool and
cloth trades, nor on the Netherlands market, important
as all these were. The city gained from the diversity of its
trade. Part of London's strength was that it was concerned
with every branch of trade and every market. The merchants of Lynn, for example, were important only in the
export of corn and the merchants of Newcastle in the
export of coal, and both suffered accordingly when the
trade in these commodities was depressed. The Lay Subsidy Rolls of 1332 show us who were then the wealthiest
merchants; in London these included not only wool and
cloth traders, but pepperers or grocers, fishmongers,

cordwainers or leather-workers, goldsmiths, pewterers, and others.

London was, in fact, so predominant in England's overseas trade that it drew to itself industrial activities even where the raw materials were not to hand, if the resulting product was in demand overseas. Thus, though London was remote from the areas that produced supplies of tin and lead, London became the chief center of the pewter industry, and in the fifteenth century a great deal of pewter ware was to be exported from London. The greatest source of alabaster in England was Derbyshire, notably the Chellaston and Tutbury mines; but by the reign of Richard II the widespread fashion for alabaster effigies and reredoses (ornamental altar screens) was redounding increasingly to the benefit of Londoners. It was London craftsmen who were mostly getting the orders for alabasters, and some of them were now doing such a large business that they were beginning to make reredoses and statues to sell from stock as soon as clients ordered them. London traders exported English alabasters on such a scale that today these objects are to be found in museums from Spain to Sweden. The threads of ecclesiastical embroidery on vestments such as copes, and the dyes to color the threads, came from a variety of sources both at home and abroad. Increasingly English embroidery, for which there was a demand throughout Europe, was made in London and sold from its shops.

All this industrial and commercial activity had a marked effect on the face of London. In the side streets of the Aldgate area and across the river in Southwark were all kinds of workshops and forges. Not all Londoners were pleased by these activities. A satirist of about 1350 complained that blacksmiths "drive me to death with the din of their dints"; and in the next century a city ordinance forbade wiresellers to work after 9:00 P.M. or before 5:00 A.M. because of the annoyance to the neighbors through their knocking and filing. To the city's smells of dung and sewage were added the sweeter scent of much charcoal and wood burning and the more acrid one of the newfangled "sea-coal," mostly brought from Newcastle and increasingly needed for the city's industries.

The more important shops were to be found in Cheapside. In West Cheap, for example, at the entrance to Foster Lane was the "Saddlery" where the saddlers and leather workers had their shops. A little farther on the right were the most famous shops in London, those of Goldsmiths' Row, which stretched from Friday Street, a street that ran roughly parallel to the east end of St. Paul's, to Bread Street farther east. It was not yet so impressive as it was to become a century later, after Thomas Wood, a goldsmith and also sheriff, had rebuilt the east end of the Row in 1491. After the rebuilding, this section, so John Stow, the Elizabethan antiquary, tells us, contained "ten fair dwelling houses and fourteen shops, all in one frame, uniformly built four stories high, beautified towards the street with the Goldsmiths' arms and the likeness of woodmen, in memory of his name, riding on monstrous beasts, all which is cast in lead, richly painted over and gilt." He thought it "the most beautiful frame of fair houses and shops that be within the walls of London, or elsewhere in England," and a few years later it even excited the admiration of a visitor from the splendid city of Venice. In the fourteenth century this row consisted mainly of low buildings of one or two stories, but they already contained considerable treasures, as may be seen from the account of two burglaries in 1382. They took place one Wednesday night in two goldsmiths' shops at the corner of Cheapside and Friday Street (so called from a Friday fish market held there). The two thieves stole several silver girdles, some silver and silver-gilt chains, and a number of silver buckles and pendants for girdles. They also took a silver chalice and paten worth 38s, two sets of silver phials (20s), a pax-bread of silver gilt (20s), two wooden cups bound with silver gilt (33s/4d), six silver spoons (14s), two gold rings with two diamonds (£15), a gold ring with a ruby (26s/8d), three strings of pearls (70s), six gold necklaces (100s), and many other articles of value worth altogether over £70, a very large amount for the time.[1] For a theft of such magnitude the offenders would have been hanged but for the fact that they were clerks and so claimed benefit of clergy, which meant they were merely shut up in the bishop's prison instead of being executed.

To export London's products and to import all the goods that the city and its hinterland needed, extensive

[1] It will help to give an idea of the value of such sums to contemporaries if one recalls that the Statute of Laborers of 1351 tried to limit a master mason's wage to 4d a day, a master carpenter's wage to 3d a day, and that in 1379 Archbishop Sudbury was trying to secure a minimum *yearly* wage for chantry priests of £4/13/4d.

wharves had already been built. They stretched continuously from the Tower to the Bridge and thence intermittently right upstream to the Fleet River. Galley Quay, just west of the Tower, was so called because it was frequented by the Italian galleys. In 1396 the Italians tried to repudiate the payment of a port toll called "scavage," but the mayor looked up the records and ruled that they must pay scavage on all goods, whether coming by land or by water. Next to Galley Quay stood the Customs House to remind the Italians and others of their obligations. A little to the west was Billingsgate, then as now the wholesale fish wharf and market. Beyond the bridge were the halls of the fishmongers and vintners, both of whom imported their wares on a considerable scale, not only for the city itself but for distribution beyond. Between them lay the Steelyard, the walled enclosure of the merchants of the Hanseatic League of North German Towns. Aware that all foreigners were growing more unpopular in an increasingly nationalist London and that their privileges and power made them especially obnoxious, they kept as much as possible behind their walls and always shut their great barred gate at night. Dominating the trade with Scandinavia and the Baltic, they were very important for the import of raw materials like pitch, tar, timber, furs, and potash (for cloth dyeing), and they took back, not only to Germany but to Scandinavia and eastern Europe, a whole range of English goods, especially dairy products, metal wares, and cloth. They and the Italians were by no means the only foreign merchants to be found in London. The visitor might also have rubbed shoulders with Flemings and Frenchmen, as characteristic in dress as Germans and Italians and equally liable to be attacked by the mob.

London's commercial pre-eminence was apparent not only in the range of its industries and shops, the extent of its wharves, or the number and variety of foreign merchants to be seen there; it was evident also in the wealth of its leading citizens. Indeed, the wealth of London merchants was such that they were becoming the government's most important normal source for loans. During the reign of Richard II we find the London merchants lending £4,000 or £5,000 at a time, usually on the security of jewels though occasionally, as in 1383, one of the king's crowns was pledged. Individuals like Sir Nicholas Brembre sometimes lent 1,000 marks at a time, and in 1397 Londoners lent (perhaps in fear) as much as 10,000 marks. Lending to the king could be risky, as he might delay repayment or even default; but it could also be very lucrative, for the king could, in return for compliance, benefit the lender in many ways. Helped by this and by their trading, some London merchants of Chaucer's day were very rich, and since they still lived in the city, London could boast some fine merchants' houses.

In the late fourteenth century some parts of London were somewhat more desirable than others. The rich wanted to have a house on or near the river front, especially at the west end of the City; the northwest of the City was also favored for wealthy residences. But the houses of richer merchants were as yet scattered in nearly every part of London. Geoffrey Chaucer's father, a well-to-do vintner, lived in the Vintry, a district bordering on the Thames and much sought by wine merchants in order to be near the wharves, especially the Three Cranes Quay where the wines were landed. Narrow lanes ran up from the wharves to Thames Street, which was parallel to the river and the main thoroughfare of the Vintry. Chaucer's father had a house in Thames Street. We have little information on what it was like, though we are told that Geoffrey ceded his claim to it in 1381; but we know from two wills what one of the adjacent houses contained. This house had two cellars, probably used for storage of both household and business goods, as was common in the houses of London merchants at this time. Above the cellars were a hall, a parlor, a bedchamber with a chimney and a closet, a kitchen with a pantry, a larder, and other offices. There were probably attic rooms as well. Such a house was not the only property owned by a merchant of John Chaucer's standing; he had at one time or another at least twenty-seven shops in different parts of the city, a brewhouse with buildings and garden attached, various other tenements, and ten and one-half acres in the fields of Stepney. All these properties were let for rent.

John Chaucer's house was by no means the grandest to be occupied by a London merchant in the fourteenth century. Sir John Poultney (or Pulteney), a draper who died in 1349 after having been four times mayor of London, had two houses, each of which was good enough for a member of the nobility. One, the Coldharbour, which he rebuilt of stone, was rented in his lifetime to the Earl of Salisbury. About 1375, Alice Perrers, Edward III's mistress, bought it; she sold it about 1390 to John Holland, Richard II's half brother, who found the house good enough to entertain the luxury-loving king there. After Holland's attainder in 1400, Henry IV lived there for a while, as did his son Henry Prince of Wales ten years later. Poultney's other large London house, called Pountney's Inn, became the home of his foundation, St. Lawrence Pountney College, whose authorities exchanged it in 1385 with Richard Fitz Alan, Earl of Arundel. In the middle of the fifteenth century it was good enough to be the London residence of William de la Pole, Duke of Suffolk, Henry VI's chief minister. But the houses of Poultney were not unique in splendor. Henry Picard, a vintner who was alderman of London from 1348–61, had a house in which he was said to have entertained five kings.

Occasionally these merchants' houses could afford the ground space to have a one-story hall, with cellars below, and a two-story structure at one end of the hall to contain a chamber and a solar above. Because of the risk of fire in a wooden building, the kitchen would in such a case be in a separate building in the backyard, over the stable. The density of population in London was, however, already causing even merchants to build in a more compact way on smaller sites. Above the cellars the ground floor in these newer houses consisted of a shop with a warehouse behind it; the hall was on the first floor, with kitchen, larder, and buttery behind it, and on the second floor were the bedrooms. As yet not much privacy was expected or provided for; as in the Reeve's Tale, the bedroom in a lesser, but not poor, household might have to accommodate not only the

master and his wife, but children and servants, visitors, or
apprentices as well. But better houses were beginning to
provide more rooms. In 1373 the inventory of the household of Thomas Mocking, fishmonger, reveals not only a
hall on the first floor, but a parlor, a chamber, and a workmen's room. In the next few generations houses were to be
brought up to date in this way. For example, in 1384 a
house on the river front between the Tower of London
and Billingsgate, leased to Richard Willysdon and his
wife, had a very large hall, forty feet long by twenty-four
wide. The house was so well built that it continued to be
occupied by prosperous merchants until the reign of Elizabeth I. Yet it had only one chamber above the hall, though
in 1384 it had a parlor, kitchen, and buttery alongside the
hall, cellars under it, and a garden and wharf so large that
eighty feet of wall was needed to extend it to the Thames.
By 1463, however, the same house had three principal
bedrooms and five garrets.

Even in Chaucer's day, however, the idea of privacy
was just beginning to creep in. Richard Lyons, the
wealthy vintner who was accused by the Good Parliament
of 1376 of corruption on a large scale at the government's
expense, had a house in the Vintry that was confiscated.
Besides cellars, shop and hall, kitchen, pantry, buttery and
larder, parlor and chapel, he had four bedrooms and two
"wardrobes" or storerooms. The privacy thus made possible was only relative; the principal bedrooms were
meant to be seen by many people. Here visitors to the
house could be impressed by the splendor and color of
the hangings and covers. Richard Lyons had in one bed-

room curtains of red-and-blue worsted embroidered with lions. His bedroom soft furnishings were not, however, as impressive as those of some other merchants of this period. The beds of Sir John Poultney had hangings and covers patterned with fleur-de-lis, eagles, lions, popinjays, and apple blossoms, in gold, blue, red, green, violet, and pink. The designs varied from leaves and griffins to wreaths of white roses on a red-and-green ground, or the story of Tristan and Isolde on a green background.

An equal brilliance of color could be found in merchants' halls. The whitewashed walls set off the woolen tapestries worked with heraldic motifs, flowers and birds, figures derived from legends like the Arthurian tales or the *Gesta Romanorum*, or with devotional representations of the Passion, the Virgin, or the Saints in colors of crimson, emerald, deep blue, orange, purple, and yellow. In the hall stood a heavy wooden sideboard, upon which for special occasions could be set an array of silver-gilt cups, mazers, and jugs, useful for displaying one's social status as well as investments which could be readily turned into cash.

Merchants were not the only wealthy men in and around London, for by Chaucer's time it was not only the greatest commercial city in England but it had become, along with Westminster, the administrative capital. The first step toward this was removal (c. 1156) of the king's chief treasury from Winchester to London in the reign of Henry II, probably because the accounting department, the Exchequer, was beginning to settle down at the palace of Westminster. Very soon afterward the judicial work of the king's court began to expand greatly, and when the common pleas, between subject and subject, started to be held in a separate stationary court, this too began to sit for convenience at Westminster. For most of the thirteenth century this custom continued: Magna Carta had promised that common pleas should be held in a fixed place, and Henry III was very fond of staying at Westminster. The practice was interrupted during the reign of his masterful son, Edward I, who wanted his government departments near at hand during his arduous campaigns for the subjugation of Scotland. For nearly seven years, from 1298 to 1305, the Exchequer and Court of Common Pleas were established at York, and even the Chancery found its headquarters there. Then, in the 1330's, Edward III sought to restore the tarnished prestige of the Crown by renewing his grandfather's aggressive policy toward Scotland. It resulted in the concentration once more of the royal administration at York, for six years from 1332–38. This had such a harmful effect on Westminster that in 1338 its householders addressed a piteous appeal to the king for a drastic reduction in their tax assessment. They said that the court and the administrative departments were their main means of livelihood and that if they were absent for long periods, as they had been in the 1330's, the men of Westminster could not make a living. A royal commission of enquiry substantially endorsed their complaints.

Relief came to Westminster with unexpected swiftness. Edward III was drifting into war with France and needed an administrative center in the south once more. So in

September, 1338, the king ordered the return of the Exchequer to Westminster "so that it might be nearer to him in the parts beyond the sea." For a few years a certain amount of administration remained at York, but as the war engaged more and more of the king's attention the struggle with Scotland was abandoned and the attempt to retain some element of the central royal administration at York faded away. A more serious threat to the pre-eminence of Westminster now arose from the practice of the king, between 1338 and 1340, of taking part of the administration with him to Flanders, so that for much of this period Antwerp became the headquarters of the king's administration in the Netherlands. But this division of the government led to confusion and may have contributed to the military fiasco of 1340. The result was that in future campaigns most of the administration was left in England and from this time Westminster became the permanent seat of an increasing number of government departments. When the Exchequer returned from York in 1339, it came back for good; it was only on rare occasions that it left Westminster thereafter.

With the Exchequer came the Court of Common Pleas, which also settled down permanently at Westminster. Soon the justices who had been hearing pleas "before the king," that is, in the royal household, drifted into the practice of sitting at Westminster. This was convenient not only for the litigants, who could find accommodation in London and consequently were spared the problem of constantly seeking fresh lodgings as the king's household went on its ceaseless wanderings. It was also useful for the judges, who could more easily consult their fellow justices of the Common Pleas and the Exchequer on tricky points. By the reign of Richard II the Court of King's Bench, as the judges sitting "before the king" had become, was usually holding its sessions at Westminster. Like the Court of Common Pleas it heard cases in Westminster Hall. Modern ears would probably find it confusing to have two law courts conducting their business simultaneously in the same hall; fourteenth-century litigants must have had to concentrate, especially as the Chancellor was with increasing frequency doing business as well in this large hall. As a great officer of the Crown he often had to be in personal attendance on the king, but though he might go to court, his staff remained at Westminster or were housed, in the case of some of the junior clerks, in nearby London. Already in 1345 the normal "place" of the Chancery was said to be that part of Westminster Hall "where the Chancellor commonly sits, among the clerks of Chancery, for exercising his office." This meant for issuing writs, but it was also coming to mean for hearing suits, as the equitable jurisdiction of the Chancellor rapidly developed.

Once administration began to cluster at Westminster on this scale, other developments followed. If petitions for redress of grievances were made, as increasingly they were, to the king's council, it would be extremely convenient if it could sit at Westminster for such business, for the councilors would readily have the advice there of the Chancellor, the judges, and the officials of the Exchequer. In 1346 a new range of buildings was erected in the palace of Westminster, next to the Exchequer of Receipt. In this range a council chamber was provided, to become famous as the Star Chamber from the decoration of its ceiling. And if Council, Chancery, Exchequer, and law courts were all meeting at Westminster, this would be specially suitable for assemblies of Parliament. It is true that most of the early parliaments had met at Westminster, but until the outbreak of the Hundred Years' War it was by no means clear that this would be the normal meeting place. Between the accession of Edward III in 1327 and the year 1338, thirteen parliaments met at Westminster and seventeen elsewhere. But between 1339 and 1377 there were thirty-one parliaments, all of them held at Westminster. By the end of Edward III's reign the Painted Chamber in the palace of Westminster had come to be regarded as the natural meeting place of a full parliament and the chapter house of Westminster Abbey was already described in 1376 as "the ancient place" of assembly of the Commons.

Parliaments were brief and irregular elements in the government of the land, but the law courts met regularly for four terms each year. As the law they administered became ever more complex, it grew increasingly necessary for litigants to have professional attorneys and pleaders. By the early fourteenth century a regular course of legal education was being provided for these pleaders, and as the common law courts were settling down at Westminster, it was natural for the legal education to be established in London, which was big enough to provide both accommodation and food supplies. It was near enough to Westminster for the law students to trudge along the muddy Strand to hear cases being tried in Westminster Hall. So began in the fourteenth century the great institutions for the training and licensing of pleaders in the common law courts, the Inns of Court, with "preparatory schools" or Inns of Chancery grouped around them.

The earliest Inn of Court to be founded may have been Lincoln's Inn, which was in existence by the middle of the century. But it has a strong rival to its claim to be the oldest Inn, for by 1347 we find part of the Temple being let to the apprentices of the law. When the military Order of the Temple was dissolved in 1311, its property in England passed to the king, who subsequently granted the London house to the kindred Order of Knights Hospitalers. The Temple in London was on the boundaries of the City of London, on the river front, and it was the part inside the city—the Inner Temple—which was let by the Hospitalers to the lawyers. By 1381 it was already so well known as a center of legal education that it was attacked by the rebels in the Peasants Revolt, for they believed that the lawyers with their parchments helped to keep the peasants in servitude. It may be that the damage done by Wat Tyler, with the consequent need for rebuilding, suggested the division of one law school into two, to cope with growing numbers. However that may be, it is clear that by the 1440's the Inner Temple and Middle Temple were firmly established as distinct institutions, though sharing a common church.

By that time the Society of Gray's Inn was also flourishing; it seems likely that the apprentices of the law became tenants of Gray's Inn by 1370. Whether any of the Inns of Chancery, for junior students, existed in Chaucer's day is not clear, though some of them, such as St. George's, Thavie's, Barnard's, Staple, Furnival, and Clifford's Inn, were certainly in existence by the fifteenth century, and Thavie's Inn and Clifford's Inn may be as old as Lincoln's Inn and the Temple.

At any rate, it is clear that Chaucer would often have met students from the Inns of Court mingling with the London crowds. Indeed, an Elizabethan biographer of Chaucer, Thomas Speght, asserted that the poet had studied law in the Inner Temple, and some modern critics have thought that the statement has some claims to credibility. Whether this is true or not, he must have seen not only law students but older lawyers whose presence contributed to the prosperity of London. Doubtless many of the "utter-barristers," young pleaders who had not long finished their training, were struggling to establish themselves and often had little to spend, but the higher ranks were men of substance.

The governing bodies of the Inns, the benchers and readers, were composed of successful lawyers, some of whom were prosperous enough to be taxed on a par with barons in the poll tax of 1379. From these successful pleaders were chosen the serjeants-at-law, who alone could represent litigants in the Court of Common Pleas. Their earnings were great; they ranked as knights and surrounded themselves with costly and elaborate ceremonies. When they were created serjeants they had to provide for their fellow serjeants and the judges a feast almost as splendid as that after the king's coronation, distributing gifts on a lavish scale and keeping up the festivities for seven days. From the serjeants the judges were chosen, and the serjeants were already consulted, along with the judges, by the government on important matters of state. They must have made a splendid sight as they walked or rode from their houses near the Inns down to the waterstairs by the Thames, thence to be rowed by ferrymen to Westminster, for serjeants were important enough to be accompanied everywhere by servants, and even the everyday dress of serjeants included a scarlet robe and cap, or coif, of pure white silk.

Lawyers were not the only men connected with the government who dwelt in the western suburbs of London in Chaucer's day. In the lane that led north from the end of Fleet Street to High Holborn the pious Henry III had, in the mid-thirteenth century, built a house for converted Jews. As the Jews were being increasingly persecuted, it is not surprising that few were ready to be converted to the faith of their persecutors, and, as the Jews were officially expelled from England in 1290, there were thereafter no Jews to be converted. The spacious buildings and chapel were therefore turned into a home for Chancery clerks and a storage space for Chancery records, to relieve the pressure on the Tower of London storerooms. By the early fourteenth century the lane outside the "house of converts" had already become known as Chancellor's or Chancery Lane, and Chancery clerks lived not only in the house itself but in the neighborhood round about. The name of the street just to the north of the present Public

Record Office (which is of course built on the site of "the house of converts") will remind us of this; in Cursitors' Lane dwelt those of the Chancery clerks who actually wrote the writs.

By the late fourteenth century they were beginning to have new neighbors in the clerks of the privy seal. In the reign of Edward I the privy seal had still been what its name implied, the private seal of the king, and its keeper and clerks had therefore naturally been lodged in the royal household. But during the reign of Edward III the clerks of the privy seal toured with the royal court less and less and stayed at Westminster more and more. One reason was that the keeper of the privy seal was coming to be specially the clerk of the king's council, and this, as we have seen, was meeting with growing frequency at the palace of Westminster. After 1360 there was a permanent nucleus of the privy seal office at Westminster even when the keeper was abroad or with the court. There was little room, however, in the even more crowded precinct of Westminster Palace for the privy seal clerks to live. Westminster village was too small and crowded, Charing village and the Strand too fashionable. It was, therefore, natural for the clerks to look for lodgings in the western suburbs of London.

At the beginning of Richard II's reign we find the clerks living in a rented house, that of the Bishop of Lichfield, or Chester as he was often known, in the Strand near the church of St. Mary-le-Strand. The keeper of the privy seal, John Fordham, was so devoted to the king that during the Peasants Revolt the mob raided this house and began to drink the wine, until they rushed away to the greater prize of John of Gaunt's palace of the Savoy, farther along the Strand. When John Fordham resigned the post shortly afterward, on the eve of his consecration as Bishop of Durham, the privy seal clerks left Chester's Inn, for the next keeper hired the inn of the Bishop of Bath and Wells near Temple Bar. But Chester's Inn was either specially suitable or particularly available, for nearly a quarter of a century later it was well established as the home of the privy seal clerks. This is clear from autobiographical references in the poetry of Thomas Hoccleve, who was a privy seal clerk and lived there with his colleagues in his bachelor days.

Hoccleve was an embittered man. He had great difficulty in getting his small salary paid, he failed to rise far in the privy seal office, he was profligate and extravagant while health and money lasted, he was in fear of dismissal as he grew older, and he found his work boring, exacting, trying to the eyes and the digestion. In spite of all this, he admits that he found good comradeship among his colleagues and led a merry life with them when he was young. They often went to the Paul's Head and Westminster taverns in the evenings, and no one complained if they were late to the office next morning. Sometimes he had enough money to hire a boat from the Strand to Westminster Palace and to treat his friends to a supper there. When he went out of his mind for seven years, from 1415–22, his salary was still paid. On his recovery he was welcomed back to his post, and a year or two later he was given a pension. More influential clerks, like those of the

Chancery, sometimes managed to get an expense allow-
ance for their journeys; and so many clerks lived in London and worked in Westminster that the government
deemed it politic to fix a maximum fare for the boat trip—
twopence per journey.

The influence of administration affected not only the
western suburbs of London but the eastern boundary as
well. The Tower of London, though physically within the
city, was a royal fortress directly under the king's jurisdiction. Because it was so strong, with fortifications that
were brought up to date in the fourteenth century by the
addition of a curtain wall with towers, it was used to store
valuables for the Exchequer and the king's household
financial office, the Wardrobe. Here at the Tower were
the factories of the king's armorers, who became more
important in the fourteenth century. Whereas previously
they had made siege engines worked by torsion, tension,
and counterpoise, now they began to make cannon and
gunpowder. These and other military supplies were kept
by the privy wardrobe. But these officials and their siege
engines and cannon were not the only signs of government
activity that Londoners of Chaucer's time would have
seen at the Tower. The king needed a few ships to act as
the nucleus of a fleet, around which could gather impressed merchant ships. The Tower served as a base for
these few royal ships and the keeper of the king's ships
had his office there. Here, too, were the king's exchanges
and the king's mint, where foreign currencies were tested
and converted into sterling coin—for a suitable fee. The
Tower's functions also provided work for Londoners, es-

pecially in the adjacent wards of Aldgate and Portsoken—
skilled tasks like the making of armor and cannon, casual
jobs like the construction of boxes for carrying arrows and
armor, or the painting of ships.

Sometimes in the fourteenth century the Tower sheltered the Great Wardrobe, the office which bought and
stored bulky commodities, such as cloth, furs, groceries,
spices, wax, and other necessities for the use of the royal
household, the king's clerks, and his army and navy. But
this was one department which found it more convenient
to take up residence in the City of London itself. The
goods it stored were increasingly bought in the city and it
became more and more difficult to find enough room in the
Tower for the Great Wardrobe and all its goods. After
various wanderings the Great Wardrobe found, in 1361,
a permanent home in the spacious townhouse of Sir John
Beauchamp, a noted captain of Edward's French wars,
who had just died. This house was near the great convent
of the Black Friars, just south of Ludgate Hill at the west
end of St. Paul's. There the Great Wardrobe remained
for three centuries until it was burned out in the Great
Fire of London in 1666. It became such a feature of the
neighborhood that the parish church of St. Andrew nearby became known as St. Andrew's-by-the-Wardrobe. The
house was big enough to accommodate the court on occasion; Richard II took refuge there during the Peasants
Revolt. Following this example other royal wardrobes
were established in the City of London. The wardrobes
of Queen Philippa and Anne of Bohemia settled in a
house called La Réole, or The Royal, in the parish of St.

Michael Paternoster, the Vintners' quarter. The Black Prince's wardrobe was established between Ironmonger Lane and the Old Jewry. The varied goods supplied to these wardrobes and the sight of their officials going about their daily business must have strengthened for Chaucer and his fellow Londoners the sense of the strong bonds linking them to the royal administration and court.

The presence of so many of the personnel of the royal courts and the royal administration undoubtedly increased the bustle and the prosperity of London in the fourteenth century, but there were also the lawyers and the clerks of the church as well. By Chaucer's day London had also become the site of the principal courts of the archbishops of Canterbury. Archbishop Pecham had moved these courts in the late thirteenth century to London, which was a much more convenient center than Canterbury for a province which stretched as far north as the Humber and the Ribble. The church of St. Mary-le-Bow, admirably sited in Cheapside, was directly subject to the archbishop's jurisdiction. Without asking permission from the Bishop of London, the Archbishop of Canterbury was able to hold his provincial courts at Bow Church—or, rather, in the crypt below it, characterized by arches that eventually gave the most important court its name, the Court of Arches. These courts grew in the fourteenth century, as did the Court of Admiralty which was closely associated with them. So in the streets of London, especially between Bow Church and St. Paul's, Chaucer would have met not only royal lawyers and clerks, but numerous officials of the ecclesiastical courts—judges, registrars, scribes, advocates, proctors. They, too, added to the wealth and importance of the city.

Besides all the government institutions and officials that were appearing on the north bank of the Thames, from Westminster to the Tower of London, in Chaucer's time there were two more developments of this kind on the south bank. In 1372, Edward III encouraged the leading men of Southwark to arrange for a building to be erected where the pleas of the steward and marshal of the royal household could be heard and where offenders against their powers could be imprisoned. The court of the steward and marshal had jurisdiction within twelve miles of the king's residence, and since the king was often in the London area, the Southwark courtroom would be in use frequently. Within these limits the court had an extensive authority—of pleas of the Crown, of debt, covenant, and trespass *vi et armis*. Londoners did not like the Court of the Marshalsea, as it was called, for they said that it sheltered culprits who had offended against the laws of the city. In 1376 they petitioned the king in Parliament to make the manor of Southwark wholly subject to their control, but Southwark was too useful to the king for him to give up his rights there. Indeed, he added to the prison of the Marshalsea of the household in Southwark a prison of the King's Bench. So Londoners had to put up with these rivals in Southwark; but it was perhaps because of their chagrin at this development that in 1394 they secured an act which brought the ward of Farringdon Without entirely under the jurisdiction of the City of London, although it was outside the walls.

The rivalry in Southwark may have been a thorn in the side for Londoners, but on the whole the development of the London region as an administrative capital in this period was much to London's advantage. It increased the prosperity which the city had long enjoyed as the social capital of England. In the twelfth century FitzStephen had noted in his description of London that almost all the bishops, abbots, and magnates of England had houses in London. If this was meant literally, then by Chaucer's day the great ones had dispersed themselves somewhat outside the walls. Early in the thirteenth century Stephen Langton, Archbishop of Canterbury, had begun to build a palace on his manor at Lambeth. Thenceforward this was the regular London residence of his successors, and a small village had grown up round it to serve the archepiscopal staff. When the Emperor Sigismund stayed at the Palace of Westminster in 1416, Lambeth Palace was sufficiently large and accessible to accommodate King Henry V and his household.

A little farther downstream on the northern bank Walter de Grey, Archbishop of York, had in 1248 acquired a fine house for his see. Known for nearly two centuries as York Place, it was seized after Wolsey's downfall by Henry VIII and renamed the royal palace of Whitehall. In this latter form it gave its name to the thoroughfare of today, but the sole remnant of the royal palace is Inigo Jones's Banqueting Hall, dating from the early seventeenth century.

Perhaps it was the combined attractions of York Place, Westminster Abbey and Palace, and the amenity of access to and from the river, with its ease of transport, which persuaded the bishops to build houses along the Strand. At any rate, by the fourteenth century almost the whole route from Charing to Temple Bar was occupied, on the river side, by the great inns of bishops, save at one important spot. This was the palace of the Savoy, so named because in the previous century it had for a while been the home of the Count of Savoy, uncle of Henry III's queen. Given to Edward I's younger brother, Edmund Earl of Lancaster, it had by Chaucer's boyhood descended to the great warrior-hero and royal favorite, Henry Duke of Lancaster, who spent a great deal of money on it. He made it so fine that it was thought a fitting palace for King John of France after his capture at Poitiers, when the English government was anxious to do all honor to him. In 1381 it suffered destruction in the Peasants Revolt. John of Gaunt, Duke of Lancaster, object of the rebels' hatred, was safely away in the north, but the rebels could storm his house and set fire to it, after piling its rich tapestries and robes in a huge pile in the great hall. Their object was vengeance, not plunder, and they are said to have hurled into the flames one of their number caught stealing away with one of the many pieces of rich plate which the house contained. The destruction was especially violent since the house had held, besides its valuables, some barrels of gunpowder which did great damage as they blew up. The palace was never rebuilt, and the site lay desolate until the sixteenth century.

The Princess of Wales, mother of Richard II, also occupied a palace outside the city, in her case right out at

Kennington. She too found it vulnerable in this time of trouble. Returning home from a round of pilgrimages to Kentish shrines, she was stopped by rebel bands marching on London, but they allowed her to leave them unmolested and she fled for refuge to the Tower of London.

But Kennington was much too far out to be convenient as a town residence, and if bishops, abbots, and priors did not have a house in a favored position along the Strand, they usually provided themselves with great houses or inns near the gate by which they would enter or leave London, to avoid traffic problems with their retinues and their baggage trains when they arrived or departed. In Southwark, near the Bridge, were the inns of several south country prelates—for example, besides those of the Bishop of Winchester and the Abbot of St. Augustine, Canterbury, those of the Abbot of Hyde Abbey Winchester and the Prior of Lewes. All together, by Chaucer's time, twenty abbots and six priors had London houses, in addition to the archbishops and bishops.

There was already a tendency for some parts of London to be more fashionable than others—Charing and the Strand, the wards of Farringdon Without and Cheap, and that of Castle Baynard, just east of Blackfriars. This ward may have derived some prestige from including St. Paul's Cathedral and the Bishop of London's Palace and from the proximity of the great house of Blackfriars, with its attached Parliament Hall where Parliament sometimes met. But the ward also had the advantage of the growing social prestige of Baynard's Castle from which it took its name. At the beginning of the fourteenth century it was known as the Old Inn and belonged to the Fitzwalter family. By the end of the century it had become the property of Richard II's uncle, Edward Duke of York, probably by marriage to Philippa, widow of Walter Fitzwalter, who died in 1386. In the next century it was to have even more distinguished owners: Humphrey Duke of Gloucester, Richard Duke of York, and the Yorkist kings. Edward IV was staying there when he received the offer of the crown, and so in turn was his brother Richard when he was offered the crown.

The movement to separate the nobility from the ordinary townsfolk by developing distinct suburbs for them in Pall Mall, St. James's, Piccadilly, Soho, and Bloomsbury did not set in until after the Civil War in the seventeenth century. In Chaucer's day great lords like the earls of Northumberland and Westmorland, Arundel and March were quite content to have houses in the City and, if need be, to hire the house of some prosperous merchant who also dwelt among the ordinary townsfolk and not in some distant suburb.

This development of London as the social capital, strengthened by its development as a commercial and administrative capital, brought not only prestige but business and prosperity. Many shops catered to residents of wealth and visitors with money. These shops varied from those of goldsmiths and jewelers who sold silver-gilt cups and rosaries of amber or jet, through turners, who offered wooden candlesticks, bowls, and cups, and scriveners and illuminators who sold illuminated books of hours or illustrated romances, to haberdashers who dealt in a great variety of luxuries and souvenirs: laces, caps, light coats, purses, spurs, chains, gaming tables, rosaries, pencases, combs, linen thread, eyeglasses, inkhorns, girdles, paper, parchment, whistles, and whipcord.

The presence of so many wealthy persons encouraged not only numerous inns and alehouses, but the existence in the Vintry, near the Thames between Queenhithe and Dowgate, of many vintners dealing in a great variety of wines, whether dry wines like those from Gascony or the Rhineland or sweet wines like those from the Levant.

The number of visitors and the wealth of many Londoners fostered the existence of a great number of pastry cooks. Their houses served not only as restaurants, in the modern style, but as shops which supplied hot food to be carried away. Many Londoners, when entertaining friends, could afford the expensive habit of sending out for their dinner ready cooked, in spite of having kitchens of their own. Particularly popular were pies containing birds—hens, geese, ducks, larks, or finches—or pies covering beef, rabbit, mutton, or venison. In the summer heat there was a great risk of these pies going bad and many were the city regulations against selling meat or pies that had been warmed up again. Cooks were naturally eager to sell their pies while they were fresh. A city ordinance of 1475 forbade pastry cooks "with their hands dirtied and fouled" to "draw and pluck other folk, as well gentlemen as other common people by their sleeves and clothes to buy their victuals whereby many debates and strifes often arise against the peace." These cooks clustered especially in Bread Street and Eastcheap. The vigorous poem, *Lon-*

don Lickpenny, long attributed to Lydgate, describes the bewilderment of a countryman dazzled by the bustle and trickery of London. The visitor goes into Eastcheap where the cooks cry their wares with deafening clatter of pots, oaths, and songs. He is pestered moreover to buy ale and wine, strawberries and cherries, pepper and saffron, hot sheep's feet and rushes, cod and mackerel, and souvenirs like Paris thread and lawn, hats and spectacles. He lacks the money to buy these wares and presently his hood is stolen. When the bargeman demands the extortionate sum of twopence to ferry him across the river, he decides that he has had enough and goes home to Kent.

Another group of crafts that benefited from the presence of so much wealth were those dealing with clothes; it was no accident that three of the wealthiest and most powerful of London guilds were those of the Mercers, the Drapers, and the Skinners. The fourteenth century was an age increasingly eager for display and pageantry, more and more anxious to flaunt richness and social distinctions in outward forms. Of these, dress offered, in that age, the greatest attractions, and it is characteristic that in 1363 the first great sumptuary law was passed, laying down what was the maximum display in clothing. For example, craftsmen and yeomen were not to wear cloth worth more than 40s a roll nor furs other than native lamb, rabbit, cat, and fox; but merchants of London who had goods and chattels to the value of £500 might wear the same quality of clothes as squires and gentlemen with lands to the value of £100 a year.

As so often with social phenomena, it is hard to tell

whether the demand preceded the technical means for its fulfillment or vice-versa, but two phenomena of the fourteenth century undoubtedly encouraged an interest in fashionable dress and contributed to the variety and gaiety of London streets. One was the rapidly growing quantity of good cloths and furs. For fine cloth supplies there were not only the great industrial towns of Flanders and northern Italy, there was the growing cloth industry of England itself. By the end of the century England was exporting ten times as much cloth as she had done in 1347–48; and Chaucer's prosperous cloth-making Wife of Bath was a common English phenomenon. Dye stuffs were being developed on a great scale and imported not only from Europe but farther afield: reds like vermilion and brasil from the tropics, kermes for scarlet from the Mediterranean, madder and weld for crimsons and yellows from Flanders, woad for blacks and brilliant blues from Picardy and Gascony. Combinations of these dyes could give other colors: brilliant greens like "Lincoln green," purples like sanguine, burnet, and murrey. Furs were coming in growing quantities, especially with the development of the Baltic trade, and these fine imported furs—ermine, lettice, squirrel, and budge—could be made a mark of social distinction, limited by the statute of 1363 to the upper classes. Great people had not one but many furred gowns; Edward III's mother owned sixteen when she died and in great households all servants of any social position were given a furred livery every year. Sir John Poultney, draper and mayor of London, knighted in 1337, had sixteen robes lined with minever or gris, fash-

ionable forms of squirrel; he also possessed fifteen un-
attached fur linings.

The attractions of this exciting range of furs and cloths
that could be dyed in all the colors of the rainbow were
enhanced by the discovery in the fourteenth century of
how to cut clothes to fit the shape of the body. This seems
to have been dependent on the invention of "cutting on
the cross" (the bias) so that cloth materials could be
stretched to cling to the body and limbs. Hitherto the
costume of both sexes had had to be loose and flowing;
from about the time of Chaucer's birth tailoring began to
be an art and the dress of the younger generation could
aim at revealing the underlying shape of the body. In a
society dominated by men and a church that preached the
importance of feminine modesty, the process could go
further and faster with young men than with girls. From
the middle of the century aristocratic young men liked to
wear tights and increasingly short jackets which also emphasized the masculinity of the wearer by widened
shoulders, padded chest, tight waist, and the short but
full skirt which contrasted excitingly with the shapely
slim hips below. By 1357 we find young Chaucer, then
aged about seventeen and a page in the household of
Elizabeth de Burgh, daughter-in-law of Edward III,
being fitted out with red-and-black tights and a short
jacket, or paltock, of this kind by a paltockmaker of London. Conservative churchmen were shocked by what
seemed to them the unprecedented lasciviousness and
luxury of the new fashions, as may be seen from the Parson's sermon in *The Canterbury Tales*, but such denuncia-

tions probably increased the daring attraction of such clothes for young gallants.

It was characteristic of the hierarchical nature of society that the sumptuary law of 1363 tried to restrict such clothes to men of noble rank; all others were to wear gowns that came below the hips. As the decades went by, the fashionable dress of young men became more, not less, exaggerated. By the 1390's the shoes had very long points, stuffed with tow, and the agelong hood had acquired a peak several feet in length which was twisted round the head into a turban, with a tail falling over the shoulder in a "liripipe." Sleeves had become so long and hanging that they had to be twisted round the arm for any task, and cloaks were "dagged" or tongued, fastened on the right shoulder with a costly clasp and thrown over the left shoulder to reveal an expensive lining. Women could share in the daring excitement of the new fashions to some extent by wearing tight sleeves and bodices of colorful, costly materials.

Toward the end of the century young and old alike could emphasize their wealth by the houppelande, a gown with a very high rufflike collar, a close fit on the bust and shoulders, vast sleeves mostly funnel shaped, a girdle (often jeweled), and very full skirts, reaching (according to the degree of ceremony required) to the knee, the calf, or the ground. This garment (worn by both sexes but especially men) had great appeal: its sleeves could be lined with expensive fur, it could be of expensive cloth, the ruff could be of a contrasting color and material (such as silk or linen), it could be worn with a costly neck chain and girdle. And it looked well with the chaperon, the turban with a liripipe and gorget (or large frill) that was often embroidered or particolored, or the high-crowned velvet hat, with a turned-up or rolled brim adorned with a costly jewel or brooch.

This development of fashionable dress was of great importance to London, for apart from the constantly moving court or other traveling great households, London was the center of fashion and in all cases the chief supplier of materials and the biggest center of tailors and dressmakers. These fashionable clothes could be immensely expensive. In the three years 1390–91, 1393–94, 1395–96 the household of Henry Earl of Derby, spent £169 on drapery, £444/9/10d on furs, and £668/15/6½d on mercery. A fashionable gown could easily cost £10 and might in extreme cases go up to £50.

The turnover for London traders from such lavish expenditure on clothes was very great. Take, for example, squirrel skins. In the year 1394–95, 79,220 skins of trimmed minever were ordered for the royal household. When Princess Philippa, daughter of Henry IV, married King Eric of Denmark in 1406, she and her escort needed 32,762 minever skins for the trousseau. Between Michaelmas, 1390, and Michaelmas, 1391, 350,960 squirrel skins were imported into London. This not only provided trade for wealthy merchant skinners, it gave employment to considerable numbers of humble men and women, especially in the districts of Walbrook, Cornhill, and Budge Row, sewing together in tiny back rooms, as fast as they could, hundreds of skins to make handsome rugs and linings, warm gloves, comfortable dressing gowns, snug counterpanes, and fur caps. The fashion trade was of sufficient importance to foster specialism in the making of clothes in Chaucer's London; we hear of cappers, wimplers, camisers (or shirtmakers), paltockmakers, hosiers, linen-armorers (for tunics worn under armor), chaucers (or shoemakers), and so on.

In trying to reconstruct the face of London we can rightly imagine, especially in main streets like Cheapside, a very colorful scene—the great lords and their retinues clad in furs and cloths of bright hues, their young men in elegantly tailored jackets and hose, and on tournament and jousting days sometimes dressed in the new and expensive plate armor which imitated, in its tight waist and shaped breastplates, the fashions of the time and gave yet more employment, in its intricate making, to London craftsmen.

We must not, however, allow ourselves to be lured into a romanticized view of London, of something like a miniature in the *Très Riches Heures* of the Duc de Berry. The city might to our eyes be picturesque in its main buildings and in its wealthier inhabitants, but it had some less pleasant aspects. In the first place it was dirty and smelly, not with the smell of petrol and the litter of paper and plastic of the modern city, but with the dirt of insanitary habits. It had a large and growing population and though the authorities tried to promote cleanliness and combat disease, they lacked both the technical and the medical knowledge to do either effectively. No adequate provision was made for either refuse collection or sanitation, and the city government fought a losing battle.

Many Londoners lived permanently on the verge of starvation and most had to work very hard for a living. They could not spare time to carry away rubbish and dung to comparatively distant places outside the walls, as required by the city authorities. So the mayor, aldermen, and council were constantly having to reiterate edicts on the subject. Thus in Edward II's time it was laid down that no person was to throw straw, dust, dung, sawdust "or other nastiness" into the streets, but in 1345 it had to be enacted that anyone convicted of throwing dirt or rubbish into streets and lanes was to be fined 2s and forced to remove it. Only nine years later the city fathers received complaints that the butchers of the Shambles were throwing the entrails of slaughtered beasts on the pavement near the Church of the Friars Minor at Newgate, so it was ordained that in future the butchers were to carry the entrails down to the mouth of the Fleet River "where the Thames ebbes and flows," regardless of the fact that drinking water was taken from the Thames. Perhaps these complaints stirred the city authorities to look again at the question of street pollution, for later in the same year they produced an ordinance "that all filth deposited before houses be removed within a week" and that "pigs be kept from wandering in the streets."

But it was of no use. In 1369 the king issued a writ to the mayor, recorder, aldermen, and sheriffs of London ordering them to pull down a jetty called Butchers'

Bridge on the Thames near Castle Baynard because of complaints received by the king's council from various notables dwelling within the City of London. It was said that the butchers were still killing beasts in the Shambles and then carrying the entrails, dripping with blood, down to Butchers' Bridge, so that "grievous corruption and filth have been generated, as well in the water, as in the streets, lanes, and places aforesaid . . . so that no one, by reason of such corruption and filth, could hardly venture to abide in his house there." The king had ordered the city authorities to provide some place outside the city where the slaughtering could be done, but his orders had not been carried out. More than two years later, in October, 1371, we find the king issuing another writ complaining that the city has still not obeyed his commands in these matters and ordering it to do so at once.

As for general street pollution, the city government in 1390 appointed Nicholas Foche as surveyor of streets and lanes within the liberty of the city "to see that they are kept clean, taking the following fines, viz., 2s from those placing filth in the streets or throwing water out of a window, and 4s from those placing filth outside their neighbours' houses. He is also to kill pigs, geese, etc., he may find at large, and sell them at the best price he can get, paying one-half of the proceeds to the Chamberlain and keeping the other half for his trouble." In hot weather the smells could be so bad that richer people often hung up bunches of herbs in their houses and held perfumed cloths or metal pomanders (like the later one now preserved in the London Museum at Kensington Palace) to their noses when they went out.

The city authorities tried to do more than forbid. By the time of Edward II they had a number of "rakyers" who were to be paid to sweep the streets by wages collected from the people of their ward by the beadles and constables of each ward. Not many towns were wealthy enough to pay for such officials, who were, however, not always as conscientious as they might have been. In 1384 the rakyer of Cheap Ward had to enter into a bond of 20s to the chamberlain of the city "not to cast or cause to be cast any dung or other ordure belonging to his own ward into the ward of Coleman Street or to throw such ordure into the kennels [gutters] during rainy weather in order that the force of the water might carry it into Coleman Street ward, and further to lead away and remove all ordure belonging to Cheap ward which was then in Coleman Street ward."

Of course, it was a problem to know what to do with the rubbish that was swept up from the streets, and six years earlier the Common Council of the city had considered the provision of places where rakyers and carters might deposit rubbish and filth. But it was hard and unpleasant work to carry these evil-smelling loads to dumps outside the city and much easier to do as the rakyer of Cheap Ward had done and push the rubbish into the next ward when he thought no one would notice. So London not only appointed rakyers but supervisors. In 1345 it was enacted that anyone convicted of dumping dirt in the

streets and lanes was to be fined 2s and forced to remove
it. Two assistants to the beadle of the ward were to be
appointed, if necessary, to see that this order was carried
out. By 1364 we hear of officials called "scavengers" who
may have been the same persons. They had full power to
survey the pavements and see that they were kept in good
repair, to ensure that the streets and lanes were kept clean,
and to report anyone hindering them in their duties.

The word "pavement" did not then mean what it often
connotes in twentieth-century Britain, if not America: a
sidewalk. There was then no distinction between roadway
and sidewalk, but in the more important streets the whole
surface was paved with cobblestones which sloped gently
to a rainwater channel in the middle of the road or, in
wide Cheapside and Cornhill, to two parallel channels
which divided the road into three sections. If rubbish was
dumped in this channel (or kennel) it would cause great
dirty pools to spread across the road in wet weather and in
dry weather the heap would stink. Whereas in 1354
householders were allowed to pile rubbish in the street in
front of their houses provided it was cleared away within
a week, by 1407 they were being ordered to keep rubbish
indoors until it could be collected by carts or rakyers.
Whether householders were willing to suffer such smelly
piles to remain in their houses or yards we do not learn.

London was not alone in these problems; indeed, many
towns appear to have had even less success in coping with
them. As late as 1402, Cambridge was prepared to allow
rubbish and dung to accumulate in the streets for seven
days, and Beverley, which in 1359 was fining burgesses

for contravening a similar rule, was a hundred years later announcing that householders would not be fined for dung heaps in the streets. But as London was so much bigger it had to make more effort, and for the same reason it did more than other towns to try to provide a clean water supply for its citizens.

The attempt was made in two ways, by prohibition and by positive action. By prohibition the city government tried to prevent the watercourses from becoming open sewers. This was a special danger with smaller streams like the Fleet River and the Walbrook. In 1355, for example, a city commission was appointed to survey the ditch surrounding the Fleet prison and to inquire who had built latrines over the said ditch and who were responsible for the accumulation of filth therein. Just over three weeks later twelve jurors were examined in the church of St. Bride's, Fleet Street. They said that the ditch was not as wide as it should have been. It ought to have been ten feet wide and have sufficient water to float a vessel freighted with a tun of wine, but it was becoming choked with sewage and the trees growing on its banks. Eleven men had, without permission, constructed latrines which contaminated the water and one of them had, in addition, built three tanneries which also polluted the river. The flow of water was so obstructed that the ditch no longer surrounded the prison as it had formerly done. It was no wonder that the death rate in the Fleet prison was always very high.

Doubtless an order was made for amendment of the river, but if so it had no lasting effect. The ground around the mouth of the Fleet River was low lying and marshy; in view of the sewage thrown or poured into the stream, the banks at the mouth of the Fleet must have been very unsavory. Already in 1290 the filth thrown into the Fleet River was creating such a stink that the White Friars, whose house stood about two hundred yards farther up the Thames, complained that the stench rose even above the scent of incense burned on the altar. Perhaps partly because of this in 1367 seven men were appointed Wardens of Fleet Bridge, whose duty it was to clean the nearby streets and lanes and the river bank. They had the right to fine any person 2s for throwing rubbish into these lanes or the river. Again their efforts were ineffective and the lower reaches of the Fleet River continued to be notorious for filth and smells until the "Great Stink" of 1858 forced Parliament to take action and provide a proper system of sewers for London.

The repellent character of the Fleet estuary meant that no one lived round it who could dwell elsewhere and it was already a resort of bad men. In 1374, Robert Duke of Brampton nightly terrorized the neighborhood by shooting arrows at passersby in Fleet Street, and desperate men were even willing to brave the mouth of the river. In 1338 two Florentine merchants journeying early in the morning between Romford and Brentwood in Essex were robbed by five thieves. The merchants turned back to London, searched everywhere, and were lucky enough to spy one of the robbers, John le Brewere, in a street. He fled to the Thames and at low tide dived in at St. Paul's Quay, hoping to escape under the shelter of the wharves to Fleet Bridge, but the tide rose and he was drowned. His body was washed up two days later on the shore of the Fleet River, near St. Bride's. In his clothing were found 160 florins and a seal taken from one of the merchants.

Bad as the Fleet River was, the Walbrook was worse. By 1383 it was said at a meeting of the Common Council that the Walbrook was stopped up by "divers filth and dung thrown therein by persons who have houses along the said course, to the great nuisance and damage of all the city." It was therefore agreed that "the aldermen of the wards of Coleman Street, Broad Street, Cheapside, Walbrook, Vintry, and Dowgate, through whose wards the said water-course runs, shall diligently enquire if any person dwelling along the said course has a stable or other house, whereby dung or other filth may fall into the same; or otherwise throws therein . . . by which the said watercourse is stopped up; . . . that so by advice of the mayor, and aldermen, and commonalty, punishment may be inflicted upon the offenders who act against this ordinance, and this nuisance be abated thereby." Nevertheless, "it shall be fully lawful for those persons who have houses on the said watercourse to have latrines over the course, provided that they do not throw rubbish or other refuse through the same, whereby the passage of the said water may be stopped. And everyone who has such latrine or latrines over the same shall pay yearly to the chamberlain for the easement thereof and towards the cleansing of the said course two shillings for each of the same. And the said aldermen are to make enquiry how many latrines there are upon the said course, and to whom they belong, and to certify the said mayor and chamberlain as to the same."

Evidently this arrangement was not satisfactory, for there continued to be complaints not only about the obstruction of the watercourse, but of the danger to health. By 1462–63 the prevalent mood had so far changed from that of 1383 that it was decided to vault over the Walbrook. Apparently there was opposition to such new-fangled notions and even in 1477 the city authorities were having to order that no latrines should be set over the Walbrook or any town ditch. But eventually the city government won, and by the time that John Stow, the Elizabethan antiquary, was writing about London, the Walbrook had long been vaulted over and paved level with the streets and lanes through which it passed. In the fifteenth century concern for the health of a growing population was shown by an order in 1415 for the demolition of one noisome public latrine, the removal of another outside the walls, and the construction of a new one near the Walbrook so that water cleansing could be effected. In 1466 a contract for ten years was made between the mayor and aldermen and John Lovegold, by which Lovegold agreed to clear all latrines for this period.

Concern for the health of Londoners did not end there. A growing city needed an increasing water supply, and by Chaucer's day this had already affected the face of London's streets. By the fourteenth century, and even in the previous century, the population was already too great for springs and wells to suffice and London had started to build conduits. Though more expensive than wells, conduits had many advantages. The water could be brought to the most convenient spot; it could be kept more uncontaminated; a constant flow could be provided at a height suitable for filling vessels; and children could be sent to draw water without fear of them falling into a well. In spite of the expense, it became a matter of public spirit for landowners to allow water to be taken from their land and for merchants to pay for conduits.

The principal source of supply was Tyburn, from which the most important outlet was erected in Cheapside at the Standard in 1285. This was naturally a great meeting place and for that reason was a favorite place of execution within the city, just as the great trees at Tyburn Springs (where Marble Arch now stands) prompted the use of them as gallows for convicts. Chaucer may well have witnessed the execution by Wat Tyler of Richard Lyons and others at the Standard in 1381. Farther east in the part of Cheap known as the Mercery was another outlet for Tyburn water, a more elaborate structure known as "the Conduit," consisting of an iron-bound lead cistern with various taps. In 1401 another conduit was to be made at the site of the old prison, the Tun, in Cornhill, the first of many conduits to be provided in the fifteenth century in various parts of the city, mainly by the generosity of leading citizens.

The city authorities were always anxious about the adequacy of the water supplies and the possible misuses of the conduits. In 1310, William Hardy took an oath before the mayor and aldermen to see that neither brewers nor fishmongers should waste the water of the conduit in Cheapside. In 1345 it was ordained by the mayor and aldermen that no brewer should use the water of the conduit for his business on pain of losing his tankard and 40d for the first offense and of being committed to prison for the third. Brewers used very large quantities of water, and fishmongers were apt to contaminate the water supply with their utensils strongly smelling of fish.

But it was not only these men who wasted water. Ordinary citizens might try to wash clothes or lengths of cloth from their looms at the conduits and, worse still, they might try to tap the conduit pipe to give themselves a private supply. In 1478 it was found that William Campion had done this and brought water to his house in Fleet Street and elsewhere. He was sentenced to be taken out of the Bread Street Compter, or "lock-up," and set upon a horse with a vessel like a conduit full of water on his head, the water running by small pipes out of the vessel. When the vessel was empty it was to be refilled. He was to be taken round the city like this and proclamation made of his misdoing; then he was to be imprisoned again at the pleasure of the mayor and aldermen. In 1367–68 the common conduit of London was leased to William de St. Albon, knight, and Robert Godwyn, cutler, for ten years at an annual rent of 20 marks, and "any of the commonalty may obtain the same water, paying for it as of old accustomed."

It was worth paying for the use of the conduit, for the alternative was to draw water from a possibly contaminated well or the even more doubtful Thames or Fleet rivers. And if householders made use of the professional water carriers, they would have to pay more for their water. These waterbearers must have been one of the familiar sights of London. The better ones took their turns at the conduits, where they were supposed to fill only one bucket at each turn to avoid causing a long queue; the more dubious ones filled up their buckets from the Thames. They were organized in a "Brotherhood of St. Christopher," and, like a modern milkman, each had a round upon which other waterbearers were not to infringe by poaching. The occupation was open to women and the mode of conveyance varied. Some carried their buckets by hand; those who were a little better off carried them in carts drawn by horses or pushed carts on wheels.

More important than the provision of either sanitation or pure water, so Chaucer's contemporaries thought, was the provision of defenses against large-scale attack and night robbers. Moreover, walls and gates were not only a safeguard for London's wealth, but a means of controlling smuggling and evasion of city tolls. The walls of London, dating from Roman times, had often been repaired and improved; indeed, the reconstruction of the section from Ludgate Hill down to the Thames on the left bank of the Fleet River was finished only in the reign of Edward II. In 1387, Richard II granted to the Londoners that tolls could be taken on wares by land and sea for ten years toward the repairing of the walls and the cleansing of the ditches that ran around them. It was especially necessary to look to the strengthening of the gates through which the city was usually entered: Ludgate and Newgate on the west side, Aldersgate, Cripplegate, and Bishopsgate on the north, and Aldgate on the east. As these gates were well fortified, they were apt to be used as prisons. When Chaucer took from the city authorities a lease in 1374 of a house over Aldgate, he secured a promise that it would not be turned into a jail during his lifetime.

Cripplegate had been a prison for debtors and common trespassers in the thirteenth century, and in Chaucer's day Newgate was one of the chief London prisons. It had become overcrowded and insanitary, encouraging attacks of jail fever. It was an act of charity for the public-spirited Richard Whittington in 1419, during his mayoralty, to persuade the aldermen to issue an ordinance re-establishing Ludgate as a debtors' prison. Ludgate prison had been abolished in June, 1419, by the previous mayor, William Sevenok, and the prisoners had been moved to Newgate. Now, in November, 1419, it was said that the atmosphere of Newgate was so fetid and corrupt that many persons had died there who might have lived if they had remained in Ludgate. In 1422, Richard Whittington left money in his will for the rebuilding of Newgate prison, which thereafter ceased to be a series of rooms over the gate and became a large building alongside it.

On the south side of the city the Roman wall had long since disappeared and the citizens relied on the fortifications at either end of the city's waterfront. On the eastern boundary stood the Tower of London, which already seemed so old and venerable that its foundation was ascribed by legend to Julius Caesar. It had been completed in essentials by the thirteenth century with two encircling walls, the inner one with wall towers, but in Chaucer's day it was still receiving minor additions such as the Beauchamp Tower, built by Edward III to house prisoners of rank.

The Tower of London could also be used as a royal residence. Richard II not only sought refuge there during the Peasants Revolt of 1381, but spent a lonely Christmas of foreboding there in 1387, after the rout of his forces by the opposition lords at the battle of Radcot Bridge three weeks earlier. He had enjoyed happier days in the Tower, such as the preparations for his coronation procession in 1377 and the grand tournament, described by Froissart, that he held there in 1390 for a large number of important foreign guests.

But the strength of the Tower had already given it fame as a sure prison for persons of great importance. David, King of Scots, was held a prisoner there after the battle of Neville's Cross in 1346, to be joined by King John of France after his capture at Poitiers in 1356. David was released in 1357, but King John had to stay in the Tower and other English prisons until 1360. Released on the conclusion of the Treaty of Brétigny-Calais, he returned to captivity in January, 1364, because of the failure to pay his ransom and the flight of his second son while on parole. The Tower was now thought too strong for him and he was lodged in the Palace of the Savoy, where he died on April 8, 1364.

About five hundred yards to the west of the Tower of London were two towers of a rather different kind, though also meant for defense: the towers on London Bridge. The wooden bridge that had spanned the Thames at this spot of firm ground had given way in the reign of Henry II to a stone bridge. It was still there in Chaucer's day and was to survive until 1831. It spanned 900 feet with nineteen arches, the piers of which were wider than the openings. Indeed, the normal width of the river was thus reduced to a waterway of 194 feet, with dangerous rapids. It was considered a very daring act to shoot under London Bridge in a boat, and many young men were drowned in trying to do so. In 1428 the Duke of Norfolk dared the racing waters in a barge, which capsized with the loss of over thirty lives. The Duke saved himself only by leaping on to the wooden starling that protected the pier of the arch.

The bridge had been provided with a chapel by Peter de Colechurch, builder of the stone bridge, and this chapel was extended and beautified in Chaucer's day, between 1384 and 1397. When he walked over the bridge, he would have caught only occasional glimpses of the river, for in the thirteenth century houses and shops had sprung up all the way along, overhanging the water to make more room inside them. A rental of 1460 lists no less than 129 tenements on the Bridge. These narrow, huddled houses made further space inside by projecting far over the roadway, turning it into a tunnel.

Toward the Southwark bank was a drawbridge protected by a tower at each end. The drawbridge, if raised, was a formidable obstacle, but the treachery of the aldermen of the Bridge ward allowed Wat Tyler and the Kent rebels to cross the bridge without resistance in 1381. That the bridge could be a formidable bulwark is shown by the successful defense that the Londoners made of their city in 1471 against the Bastard of Fauconbridge by resisting him at the drawbridge. At this point traitors' heads, hoisted on poles on the top of the northern tower of the drawbridge and slowly yellowing into skulls in the wind and rain, were a grim warning to riotous persons not to attempt to attack the chief city of the realm. After 1393 travelers arriving from Southwark were further reminded of the royal majesty by the erection of stone effigies of Richard II and Queen Anne, set in tabernacles on the Great Stone Tower to the north of the drawbridge.

Farther west along the river bank stood the great fortified enclosure of the Hanseatic merchants, the Steelyard, on the site of the present Cannon Street Station. Half a mile farther west there had been, in Norman days, two strongholds on the edge of what was then the city wall, presumably to dominate the entrance to the Fleet River. These two were Montfichet's Tower and Baynard's Castle, but by Chaucer's day they had long since disappeared in the precincts of the great Blackfriars Convent. By the early fifteenth century a house a little to the east, the Old Inn, had acquired the name of Baynard's Castle, but it had no connection with the former stronghold except a tenuous family one. Just to the west of it a tower had been built by Edward I and Edward II, perhaps to guard the Fleet River, but Edward III had granted it to Lord Roos and in Chaucer's day it seems to have played no part in London's defenses.

The fact was that by the fourteenth century there was no longer any need to rely on private strongholds for the defense of London, for the civic authorities were anxious to have full control of this essential task. The city government took seriously the work of defense of the walls, gates, and bridges. In 1377, when Edward III was dying and the French were threatening invasion, ordinances were made for the safeguarding of the city. The gates were to be fortified with portcullis and chains and a barbican in front; the quays between the Tower of London and London Bridge were to be barricaded; the aldermen of the riverside wharves were to array the men of their wards; the aldermen of the bridge were not only to guard it but provide ordnance of stone and shot. The aldermen of the outer wards were to look to the defenses of their own section of wall and ditch and gate, if any, while the aldermen of the inner wards were to muster their men as a mobile reserve.

But even in more peaceful times the city made arrangements to defend the walls and gates. By an ordinance of 1321 the aldermen were supposed to provide twelve strong men, well armed, to guard each gate during the day and twenty-four men each night. The great gates were to be shut at sunset by their warders and the wicket gates could stay open only until curfew was rung at 9:00 P.M. on the bell of St. Martin-le-Grand. Then even the wickets were to close for the night, to be reopened when prime was rung at St. Thomas of Acon. The great gates were to be opened at sunrise. Every night a watch of two hundred men was to patrol the city to keep the peace and help the watchers at the gates if need be. In addition, every alderman was to see that there were enough able-bodied men on watch in his own ward to keep order there during the night. Two good and strong boats with armed men were to watch on one side of London Bridge and two other such boats on the other.

All these precautions show the dread of the governing classes of attack from outside the city and violence and theft within it during the hours of darkness. This was not surprising, for on moonless nights it was only too easy for the attacker or thief to escape along the maze of lanes and alleys, shrouded in darkness intensified by the narrowness of the streets and the overhanging houses. In winter they could be pitch black. As a precaution against such dangers the law was that no man should be abroad after curfew unless he was of good repute and could show good cause, and even then he was subject to strict rules about the bearing of arms and ought to carry a light to show that he was an honest man.

The dangers of attacks in the dark and of rubbish in the streets are both illustrated by a murder on a January night in 1322. Just before midnight John de Tygre was attacked in Soper's Lane by an enemy named John de Eddeworth, who was aided by two other men. Tygre fled from street to street, but in Wood Street he fell over a heap of dung and was promptly wounded many times with a sword and so beaten with a staff that he died a few days later.

From time to time a concession was made by proclamation that people might be out until ten o'clock at midsummer, but for the rest of the year the time to be indoors was by curfew: nine in summer, eight in winter. In an age when no one owned a watch and clocks were a rare public amenity, four city churches were officially designated as ringers of the curfew. These were St. Mary-le-Bow in Cheapside, All Hallows Barking in Tower Ward, St. Bride's in Fleet Street, and St. Giles outside Cripplegate. In 1370 it was enacted that no one was to wander in the city after curfew had sounded at these churches, which replaced such churches as St. Martin-le-Grand where curfew had earlier been sounded.

After curfew all noisy work, such as the knocking and filing of the wiredrawers, had to stop so that the neighbors could get to sleep. After this hour the watch would not only patrol the streets but visit inns and hostels if the alderman of the ward thought fit, for strangers and inn frequenters, it was thought, might include persons of dubious character who might be especially prone to wander out after nightfall to commit theft or violence. Any person accosted at night by the watch and unable to give an account of himself was liable to arrest (especially if he was not carrying a light), to spend the night in one of the Compter prisons (or "lock-ups") and to appear before the mayor in the morning.

The task of maintaining order was increased, paradoxically, by the piety of past and present generations of Londoners. One striking feature of the face of London, which would certainly impress a modern observer and even struck visitors in the fourteenth century, was the number and wealth of its churches. This, together with the social and legal position of the clergy at that time, had two important consequences for order. One was that clerics were extremely numerous; not all were devout or even peaceful, yet all enjoyed benefit of clergy and it was extremely difficult for the city authorities to deal with the riotous behavior of clerics. It has been calculated that there were at least ten times as many clerics in proportion to the population in fourteenth-century England as there are today, and many of the clerics of that time (especially those in minor orders) lacked the sense of dedication which usually characterizes the clergy of the present day.

Clerical privilege meant that, except for treason, the clergy were much less severely punished than the laity for the same crime. The parsons of London livings tended at this time to change benefices with unusual speed and some of them at least cannot have shown the concern for their flocks that Chaucer's poor parson displayed. St. Botolph's Bishopsgate, for example, had at least fifteen rectors between 1362 and 1404. Added to this was the fact that London, as the capital and a relatively big city, attracted a considerable number of lawless clergy from other places, many of whom were seeking to make money by the exchange of livings, as Archbishop Courtenay complained in a mandate of 1392 against "chop-churches."

All this meant that clerics were often involved in the stabbings and brawls which so frequently occurred in London in this century. Thus in 1324 a knight and a rector, on their way to see the Bishop of Bath and Wells, quarreled with each other. They drew their swords, and the rector inflicted on the knight a mortal wound on the right side of his head. Two years later a chaplain visited his mistress in the parish of St. Lawrence Jewry and found her with another lover; he stabbed his rival to death with a sword in the stomach, the woman abetting him. In the reign of Richard II clerics in London were found guilty of offenses such as clipping coin, robbery, manslaughter, and murder. In view of clerical immunity it was difficult enough for the coroner and sheriffs of London to deal with such cases when they occurred in the city. In Southwark, where there was no over-all authority, violence was endemic. Sometimes fairly high-ranking clerics were involved, as when the prior of Bermondsey, with a monk and three other men, broke into a house in Southwark, assaulted the occupant, and carried away his goods.

The other feature of the Church that worked against the enforcement of order in London was the right of sanctuary. In canon law any consecrated building provided refuge for the fugitive and it was sacrilege to lay hands on him within the consecrated "House of God." Sometimes people even tried to use parish churches for this purpose, but that could be a weak protection. Thus in 1321 a woman who had killed a clerk of the church of All Hallows, London Wall, and tried to seek refuge in the church, was repudiated by the Bishop of London. She was dragged out and taken to Newgate prison, where she was hanged three days later. It was a different matter with the greater churches which enjoyed chartered rights, and there were many such in and around London. (More will be said about these greater sanctuaries in the next chapter, when we come to ecclesiastical jurisdiction.) Great churches like Westminster Abbey, St. Paul's

Cathedral, and St. Martin-le-Grand were not only refuges for criminals and swindlers, but bases for the continued operations of such felons, especially by night when they could sally forth and then retreat to sanctuary before dawn.

Though the unruliness of many of the clergy caused anxiety to the city authorities and occasioned friction between them and the Church's dignitaries, clerical violence was not the most prominent aspect of the Church from the point of view of the visitor to London. What struck him at once was the number and splendor of the churches. The remarkable devotion of Londoners in earlier generations, especially those of the eleventh and twelfth centuries, had bequeathed to Chaucer's London well over 120 parish churches. Why this situation should have arisen is a puzzle which Professor C. N. L. Brooke has recently investigated and one which would take too long to explore adequately here.[2] It will not do simply to murmur "Ages of Faith" as an explanation. Ely had only one parish church, Hull only a chapel-of-ease, whereas London probably had more parish churches than any other town in Christendom, one for every three and one-half acres. Many of them may have originated as neighborhood churches, built by groups of neighbors expressing a devotion to a particular saint; but if so, it was all the more remarkable that so few of them, after several centuries of existence, seem to have become neglected. On the con-

[2] See C. N. L. Brooke, "The missionary at home: The Church in the towns, 1000–1250," *Studies in Church History*, edited by G. J. Cuming, Vol. 6 (C.U.P., 1970), 59–83.

trary, during the century and a half before the Reformation over half the London churches were rebuilt or enlarged. When the old church of St. Stephen Walbrook was found to be too small and incapable of enlargement, an entirely new church was built on another site in 1428. By Chaucer's day most of the London churches had one or more chapels added to them, and many had three or four. At the altars in these chapels, or at altars down the nave itself, were said or sung masses for the members of the numerous fraternities or guilds. On a summer's morning the visitor to London would have heard from about four or five in the morning until about nine a constant succession of church bells tolling for the celebration of "morrow" masses. When he had dressed and gone out into the streets, he would have heard, at almost every second or third street corner, the murmur of a parish or a chantry mass through the open door of a parish church.

But the parish churches, though so numerous, were by no means the only religious edifices the traveler would have encountered in and around the city. On many of the roads into London he would have been made aware of the power of the Church and of the extensive lands of great religious bodies even before he entered the city. On the southwest was Westminster Abbey with its wide estates at Covent Garden and elsewhere in the area; on the northwest was the large area just outside Aldersgate occupied by the Priory of St. John of Clerkenwell, the Charterhouse, and the Priory of St. Bartholomew; on the northeast were Bethlehem Hospital and the Priory of St. Mary Spittle. On the east, by the Tower of London, stood the Cistercian Abbey of St. Mary Graces, founded by Edward III to honour Our Lady of Graces in gratitude for his escape from many perils by land and sea. To the north of the abbey lay the Franciscan house of Minoresses, much patronized by the nobility in Chaucer's day. Just by the abbey, on the river front, was the extensive precinct of St. Katharine's Hospital, in which Edward III's wife, Philippa, took a keen interest. As a young man Chaucer would have seen much building activity on both abbey and hospital. Finally, the traveler approaching London from the south could not fail to be aware of the importance and influence of the Abbey of Bermondsey and the Priory and Hospital of St. Mary Overy at Southwark. Chaucer's fellow-poet John Gower spent the last years of his life in the precincts of the priory and was buried in its church.

Within the city itself the traveler was confronted with still more important religious foundations. If he entered by Aldgate he would at once have seen on his right the impressive church of the Augustinian Priory of Holy Trinity, much favored by Matilda, queen of Henry I, and endowed with the property of the most ancient guild in London, the "Cnichtengild." Stow describes the church as "very fayre and large"; it was a loss to London when it was destroyed at the Reformation. The church of the nearby nunnery of St. Helen's in Bishopsgate Street, founded for daughters and widows of London citizens, was to be more fortunate and to survive as the parish church of St. Helen's Bishopsgate. Farther west, in Cheapside, was the large Hospital of St. Thomas of Acon,

founded by the sister of St. Thomas Becket, which com-
memorated him and also functioned as a hospital. If
the traveler put up at one of the neighboring inns, he
would be reminded early in the morning of the existence
of this hospital's church situated at the corner of Old
Jewry, for the hour of prime, rung upon its bell, was the
signal for all gates to be opened to traffic.

London enjoyed the services of more than a dozen hospitals, some for the sick, some for the poor and aged.
Other general hospitals were St. Bartholomew's, St. Mary
Spittle without Bishopsgate, having one hundred beds,
and St. Thomas at Southwark. There were also special
hospitals. Papey Church, by the city wall just north of
Aldgate where Chaucer lived at one time, was a home for
priests disabled by age or sickness. St. Mary of Bethlehem
was a small hospital chiefly for the insane. Elsing Spittle,
near Cripplegate, founded in 1329 by William Elsing, a
mercer, was for one hundred blind men, while the Lock
Hospital in Southwark and St. James's Hospital at Charing, on the site of the present St. James's Palace, were for
lepers.

The traveler who entered the city from the western
end, via Holborn, would also have encountered a large
and splendid church as soon as he had passed through the
city wall, the church of the Greyfriars in Newgate. In
Chaucer's day the magnificent church, three hundred feet
long and eighty-nine feet wide, which aroused the admiration of all who saw it, was still new. Noted for its fine
stained glass windows, it had been raised by the piety of

three fourteenth-century queens—Margaret, Isabella, and Philippa—and was provided with sumptuous choir stalls in 1380 by the Countess of Norfolk. In 1429 the executors of Richard Whittington enriched it with a large library, with twenty-eight desks and eight double settles. Edward I's second queen, Margaret, was buried in the Greyfriars Church, and this seems to have started a fashion. The queens Isabella and Joan of Scotland were also buried here, as well as many members of the aristocracy and leading merchants of London, so that by Chaucer's day the tombs were part of the wonder of the church.

If anyone entered the city by Ludgate, he would find another extensive and equally impressive house of friars just inside the city wall. This was the Blackfriars, the house of the Dominicans, who had found a powerful patron in Hubert de Burgh when they first came to England in 1221 and had in consequence been granted a striking site opening on to Ludgate Hill and stretching nearly to the river front. The London Blackfriars remained so influential that it absorbed Montfichet's Tower and Baynard's Castle and even obtained permission to move forward a portion of the city wall to the bank of the Fleet River so as to enlarge the by now rather cramped site. Its hall was so big that occasionally Parliament met there, and the Emperor Charles V was to lodge at Blackfriars when he came to England. The house of the Austin friars in Broad Street was less striking, but its church was good enough to be preserved at the Reformation as the church of the Dutch Protestants. At the eastern end of the city, near the Tower, stood the house of the Crutched Friars, in Hart Street, and between Fleet Street and the river was the extensive convent of the White Friars.

All these parish, monastic, and friary churches and hospitals made a very forceful testimony to the power of the Church over men's minds at that time, but in addition there was the most impressive building of them all, St. Paul's Cathedral. With an internal length of 560 feet, it was longer than the present St. Paul's, and it was 86 feet wide with transepts extending to 290 feet. Most people find the height of Wren's cathedral awe inspiring; but the height of the present cross on the dome above the pavement is 365 feet, whereas the height of the top of the spire of Old St. Paul's above the ground was 489 feet. The tower rose 285 feet and the spire measured another 204 feet. The church as it stood in Chaucer's day was largely a creation of earlier centuries, especially the thirteenth. In the early years of that century the clerestories of the nave were added, and by 1221 the tower and its timber spire were finished. In 1256 the remodeling of the east end from Norman into Gothic was begun. It resulted in an eastern arm of twelve bays, the longest and one of the finest in the land, with a magnificent rose window in the east wall 40 feet in diameter.

The most important contributions of the fourteenth century to the church itself were the new pedestal of the shrine of St. Erkenwald, started in 1314, the replacement of the spire in the next year, and, in midcentury, the addition of a solid stone screen, or pulpitum, with a great rood at the entrance to the choir. Of greater importance architecturally were the cloisters and chapter house, begun in 1332 by Walter de Ramesey, who for six years had been working in St. Stephen's Chapel at the Palace of Westminster. At St. Stephen's and St. Paul's he probably evolved the Perpendicular Gothic style which was to be so important for English architecture over the next two centuries. The stiff tracery of the chapter house and upper cloister windows, the mullions continued as paneling, and the rectilinear paneling are all early examples of Perpendicular art. The last addition of this century was the new front of the south transept carried out under the supervision of Henry Yevele, the famous mason of Westminster Abbey, who received his last payment for the work in 1388.

The visual impact of St. Paul's was not limited to the church itself, for at that time it was surrounded by a large churchyard enclosed by a high wall. Within this churchyard were the bishop's palace (containing a great hall where the bishop entertained kings, nobles, and foreign potentates), the deanery, the houses of the thirty greater canons, and, from the early fifteenth century, the college of the minor canons who were incorporated in 1395–96. Also within the precinct was the common hall of the many vicars, who deputized at the ordinary services for the canons, the famous open-air pulpit of St. Paul's Cross at the northeast, and a detached bell tower at the east end. At the southwest angle of the cathedral was a parish church and at the northwest angle was the bishop's palace. Between this and the north transept was the cloister called Pardon Church Haugh, in the garth of which stood a chapel founded by Gilbert Becket, father of the patron saint of London. Because of this and Gilbert's tomb there, the chapel attracted much attention. Many famous people were buried there, the city authorities made processions to it, the cloister was to be rebuilt in Henry V's reign with a series of thirty-six allegorical paintings of the Dance of Death, and in his son's reign it was to be provided with a fine library on the upper floor. To the north of the Pardon Church Haugh was later built the College of Minor Canons and to the east of this college was the Charnel House, where the bones of many thousands of Londoners were stored. In 1379 the Fraternity of All Souls was formed to maintain the chapel, which became the burial place of several noted citizens, including at least three mayors.

The visitor to a cathedral close in modern times may be tempted to think of St. Paul's and its churchyard as a place serene and withdrawn from the traffic outside. This was not the case. Sermons were preached to large crowds at the famous cross in the churchyard, and from its pulpit proclamations were read and statutes proclaimed. The belfry announced the hours of services, but it also called citizens to arms. The churchyard was used for arbitration meetings in disputes and an assembly of this kind was held in 1318 between Edward II and his barons. In spite of repeated prohibitions, Londoners used the churchyard for wrestling matches and games and the interior of the church was equally profaned. At the west end sat twelve scriveners, ready to compose documents for officials, merchants, and anyone else who came with money. Within the aisles the serjeants-at-law stood to await employment by litigants, each having his allotted pillar as a recognized rendezvous. Tradesmen set up stalls in the cathedral, and in 1385 Bishop Braybrooke condemned the practice in vain. Indeed, one pillar was marked with a standard measure for the benefit of traders. The transepts were a recognized thoroughfare from north to south, not only for ordinary pedestrians but for porters or merchandise. In the late mornings and the afternoons the cathedral must have been full of bustle and noise, the chief meeting place of London.

Yet it must also be remembered that many people came to pray, not only at the shrine of St. Erkenwald but at the altars. It has been estimated that the offerings of pilgrims at the shrine in the mid-fourteenth century amounted to £9,000 a year and much devotion was shown to the Great Rood at the entrance to the choir and the miraculous Rood at the north door. There was also veneration for the numerous relics, which included a knife of Our Lord, a hand of St. John the Evangelist, some hair of St. Mary Magdalene, a piece of Becket's skull, all preserved in jeweled reliquaries.

In the early morning, mass was regularly said at over thirty altars, and the cathedral was bright with candles and colorful vestments. At the end of the fourteenth century there were more than 70 perpetual chantries in the cathedral, as well as 111 obits and innumerable bequests for occasional masses. To serve all these there was not only an army of chantry priests but several guilds. People also came to look at the tombs of Saxon kings, bishops, deans, nobles, and knights. One of the most splendid tombs was that immediately north of the high altar, the tomb of John of Gaunt and his first wife, Blanche of Lancaster, in memory of whom Chaucer wrote his *Boke of the Duchesse*. Chaucer would have been able to watch this tomb in the making. In 1374 he was appointed controller of the customs of London and took up residence at Aldgate, and it was in that year that John of Gaunt gave instructions to his agent at Tutbury in Derbyshire to dispatch six cart-loads of alabaster for the tomb and two special blocks for effigies of himself and Blanche. Henry Yevele, famous master mason of Westminster Abbey, was paid lavishly for the effigies, which were eventually surmounted by a canopy of elaborate Perpendicular tabernacling. Every September, on the anniversary of Blanche's death in 1369, an anniversary mass was sung at her tomb. Professor C. S. Lewis has suggested that Chaucer's elegy may first have been read before an audience after the service in September, 1374, when the duke was able to attend for the first time.

So we see some of the leading characteristics of London as they presented themselves to the visitor in Chaucer's day: the town in close touch with the countryside, the busy market town, the thriving commercial city, the center at Westminster of administration and law, the magnet of society and fashion, the city of pollution and violence, the city of wealth and of churches. But to appreciate adequately the London influences on Chaucer's life we need to understand something of London's government and the quality of London society. To the first of these we now turn.

84

III

The Government of London

By the time of Chaucer the government of London was as complex as its appearance. This age was of crucial importance in settling the form and character of London's government for many generations to come.

By the beginning of the fourteenth century London was not only independent of the ordinary shire administration, but was normally free from direct royal interference. King John had restored to London the right to elect its sheriff and had granted it the right to choose its mayor each year. On a number of occasions, however, Henry III and Edward I had taken the government of the city into their own hands; this had culminated in Edward I's suspension of the city's self-government for thirteen years, from 1285–98. Thereafter, however, it was only rarely and for brief intervals that the city government was overridden by the king. Edward III, grateful for London's support, granted in his first charter of 1327 that the city's constitution should not be suspended because of the conduct of private individuals or even of individual officials of the city. When Richard II appointed a warden and took the government of London into his hands in 1392, his act was bitterly resented because it was the first time such a thing had happened for seventy years. The memory of it was a strong factor in the support given by Londoners to Henry Bolingbroke in 1399, and in 1400 the new king responded with a statute intended to safeguard London from unjustified interference in its government. London's relative freedom from royal intervention in the fourteenth century meant that internal dissensions could have full play; and these stresses were both numerous and strong.

The mayor was assisted in the government by twenty-four aldermen, one for each of the wards into which the city had been divided since at least the twelfth century and perhaps earlier. So far from being elected in modern fashion by the residents of the ward, the aldermen of the early thirteenth century usually held their position by hereditary right, as members of a closely related group of sixteen patrician families. The alderman exercised much control in his ward by setting the watch and guarding the walls and gates (if any) in his ward and by holding a "wardmoot" which had considerable police and judicial powers. The control of the city by a small knot of patricians had come to be resented by the middle of the thirteenth century. Henry III was disturbed in his last illness by the noise of the "have-nots" of London rioting against the "haves" in the election of the mayor. The patricians had not much to fear from the laboring classes who, though numerous, were unorganized and poor, but the rising craft guilds were another matter.

As the premier town in the kingdom increased in size and importance, there was growing incentive for specialization in trade and industry and an increasing urge of those engaged in any rising craft to organize themselves in a guild. The craft guild not only claimed to control its craft but was very exclusive; not only was the "foreigner," the outsider or non-Londoner, to be shut out, but no one within London was to be permitted to work at any trade or manufacture unless he belonged to the guild that claimed to control his craft. The guildsmen bitterly resented Edward I's attempts to protect alien merchants and promote trade between aliens and nonfreemen. It increased their determination to break into the city government and to protect their interests. This provoked the initial hostility of the city authorities who saw in it a challenge to their claims to control all trade and industry within the city, but before the end of the thirteenth century many of the craft guilds were becoming so strong that the mayor and aldermen were forced to recognize their existence and in some cases to approve their organization.

By the early fourteenth century the power of the craft guilds had so increased that in 1311 we find a reforming mayor granting rights of self-regulation to many crafts, with the support of the aldermen. But this was no longer enough; the craft guilds wanted a share in the city's government and they began to get it. They wanted the rights of citizenship to be protected against immigrants and other nonfreemen. Improved records and a more efficient bureaucracy enabled them to make a drive to ensure the registration of freemen and payment of taxes; over nine hundred men were enrolled as citizens between 1309 and 1312. In 1319 a charter which the city obtained from Edward II laid down that no stranger should be admitted to citizenship unless his claim was supported by six men of the craft he wished to follow; the same charter enacted that the mayor and aldermen should be annually elected. The subsidy rolls of 1319 show that the wealthiest merchants were drapers, mercers, grocers, fishmongers, woolmongers, skinners, and goldsmiths, the kind of merchants who were later to form the dominant group of the twelve great livery companies. A quarter of a century later a Common Council had been organized with considerable powers of administration and legislation for the city. This council was elected by wards, each ward sending four to eight members, according to its size. The usual method of acquiring freedom of the city and hence voting rights was now to be a member of a craft guild, which meant the guilds would be well represented in the Common Council. This was not enough, however, for the stronger guilds.

The number of guilds increased and by the end of the reign of Edward III had risen to eighty-eight, but the growth of London's commerce meant that the trading guilds, or those in which the trading element predominated, became of greater importance as compared with the handicraft guilds. The trading guilds were not content with the limited privileges which could be obtained from the mayor; they began to apply to the king for royal charters. A lead was given by the Goldsmiths, Skinners, Taylors, and Girdlers, who obtained royal charters in 1327. They were followed in 1363–64 by the Drapers, Fishmongers, and Vintners. These early charters varied in detail, but all gave to the petitioners a monopoly of their trade and the right to see that proper standards were enforced, a function that had hitherto belonged to the mayor and sheriffs. The guildsmen also gained power to punish any breach of their privileges and control over their members. These important trading guilds not only bought royal charters, but were so influential by the second half of the fourteenth century that they began to enroll nobles, bishops, and even kings among their fraternity.

It is not surprising that the stronger guilds wanted more power, and in 1351 the thirteen greater guilds were invited to choose members of their craft to act as the Common Council of the city. In 1353 the election of the Common Council was restored to the wards. It is at first sight a paradox that in 1376 reformers should have wanted the elections to be by guilds again. The fact was that the number of guilds had increased greatly by that time, including many lesser craft guilds of less wealthy men, and the reformers hoped that by this means the domination of the city government by wealthy guildsmen, especially victualers, would be broken. But just because of this the great trading guilds, especially victualers like grocers, fishmongers, and vintners felt that election by guildsmen would give undue influence to lesser craftsmen; they were confident that they could hope to control a ward election based simply on citizenship.

In 1384 the victualing interests secured the restoration of election to the wards and after that date the Common Council was usually dominated by leading members of the more important guilds. Moreover, the same constitution of 1384 laid down that the election of the mayor and sheriffs should be in the hands of the Common Council "with as many sufficient men of the city as they might think necessary." This was interpreted to mean the more important members of the greater guilds. From 1394 aldermen were to hold office for life and be chosen by the mayor and aldermen from two persons nominated by the ward. Since the aldermen were by this time members of important guilds, this rule consolidated the power of the trading guilds. Henceforth, until 1649, there is no instance of the election of a mayor who was not a member of one of the more powerful trading guilds, such as the Mercers, Drapers, or Grocers.

By 1400 London had a firmly established merchant oligarchy. In theory its control was subject to the concurrence of the Common Council, in which the interests of the minor guilds could find a place, and there could be at times clashes within the dominant class, as when Taylors and Drapers came to blows in the Guildhall over the election of the mayor in 1440. But until the eighteenth century the fundamental control of the merchant oligarchy over the city's government was never seriously challenged after the reign of Richard II (save, as Dr.

Valerie Pearl has shown, during the troubles of the Civil War).

This era of comparative stability was not achieved without bitter strife in the reign of Richard II among the trading guilds themselves. In the thirteenth century Londoners had been to a considerable degree dependent on the activities of alien merchants, but by the middle of the fourteenth century many English merchants, like Thomas Swanland, Walter Cheriton, or John Poultney, had accumulated capital to such an extent that Edward III increasingly relied on them to finance his war in France. These merchants were engaging in foreign trade on a growing scale and wanted to exclude the foreign merchant from the London market. In this aim the greater victualing guilds—the Grocers, Fishmongers, Vintners—were only acting in the same spirit as the others, but the effect of their attempts at monopoly of the food supplies was to raise their price and produce a scarcity from time to time. This aroused the hostility of the exporting interests, such as mercers and drapers, who wanted to keep down the price of food for their workers. Their attitude was illogical, for they wished to maintain their own monopolies, but they sought popular support against the victualers.

Naturally the support of the laboring classes could be aroused for a policy of cheaper food and drink, and the members of the lesser guilds, together with the humbler employees of the great guilds, were pleased to strike a blow against some of the richer merchants who dominated London's government. On the other hand, some of the smaller craftsmen, such as weavers, resented the attempts of the great traders in cloth, such as drapers, to make London a depot for all sorts of English cloth and to encourage the influx of Flemish weavers. The situation was conducive to a clash and to the emergence of a leader from among the ruling class who could win support from the nonvictualing guilds and from the laboring populace.

Such a man appeared at the end of Edward III's reign in the person of John of Northampton, draper and alderman. His immediate followers were a draper, two mercers, a merchant tailor, and a goldsmith; he found support as well among saddlers, cordwainers, haberdashers, and members of lesser crafts. He accused the victualers of trying to raise the price of imported foodstuffs and in 1377, the year of the old king's jubilee, he secured the compilation of a Jubilee Book of ordinances which dealt especially with the sale of victuals, to secure as much free trade as possible. His opponents were able and united and appealed skillfully to public opinion by a combination of lavish display, denunciation of the restrictive practices of the drapers and mercers, and an appeal to antiforeign prejudices.

Soon after the accession of the young king, victualers became predominant in the city government—men like William Walworth and Walter Sibil, fishmongers, John Philpot and Nicholas Brembre, grocers. Walworth and Philpot were appointed treasurers by Parliament to ensure that its recent grant was all spent on the French war. John of Gaunt, whose influence predominated in the government, resented this control by mere merchants. His hostility to them was increased by the contrast between the failure of his own expeditions to France and the success of the private fleet fitted out by Philpot for action against the pirates in the Channel who were so harmful to trade. Knowing John of Gaunt's enmity toward the victualers, John of Northampton allied himself with Gaunt. In the Parliament of October, 1378, the duke got Walworth and Philpot removed from their office as war treasurers and the monopoly of the victualing trades in London was destroyed by a statute that allowed free trade in all foodstuffs except wine.

The victualers naturally hit back. To gain favor in London they declared that the trading privileges of Londoners, great and small, were being threatened by foreigners and that London's freedom was being attacked by the duke. By these means they ensured that victualers continued to be chosen as mayor, John Philpot in 1378, John Hadley, a pepperer, in 1379, William Walworth in 1380. But their incitement of attacks on aliens had displeased the government, and a rumor arose that the king intended to make Southampton the chief center of the Italian trade instead of London. In turn this stimulated the murder of a Genoese in a London street by John Kirkeby, a Londoner. The government was determined to punish him and London. He was condemned to death, not at a Parliament at Westminster, but one held at Northampton, which therefore deprived London of the customary trade from a meeting of Parliament. This same Parliament enacted the fatal poll tax which triggered off the Peasants Revolt.

The revolt proved to be a serious blow to the power of the London victualers. It is true that in the final stages, when the young king was faced with the ugly situation at Smithfield, created by the killing of Wat Tyler, Mayor William Walworth acted with courage and resolution. Next to the king himself, he did most to save the situation, and with John Philpot and Nicholas Brembre he was knighted by Richard immediately afterward. But in the previous days the city authorities had not only been supine in the face of rioting, plundering, and murder, some of the victualers were charged with aiding the rebels out of spite against the recent actions of the government toward London. Alderman John Horn, a fishmonger, was accused of encouraging the rebels, giving them a royal standard to display on their march and lodging some of the leaders in his house. Alderman Walter Sibil, fishmonger, was said to have opened London Bridge to the men of Kent, and Alderman William Tonge, vintner, was charged with admitting the men of Essex through Aldgate.

It seemed suspicious that the rebels should have been so concerned to sack the Duke of Lancaster's palace, the Savoy, and above all to search for the Jubilee Book, which did not concern them but did affect the victualers. These accusations and suspicions did grave damage to the cause of the victualers, and in the mayoral election of October, 1381, their great foe, John of Northampton, was elected mayor. In the Parliament that met in October, 1382, he secured a statute which forbade victualers to hold judicial office in any town, prohibited them from buying most kinds of fresh fish for resale, and threw open both whole-sale and retail trading to foreigners. He also made the fishmongers bring their charters to the Guildhall to be scrutinized, and victualers found selling defective food or short measure were severely punished, either by confiscation of the offending stock or standing in the pillory or both. He kept a sharp watch for any opposition to his rule, and any criticism was at once punished. Nicholas Exton, a fishmonger, was deprived of his aldermanry and banished from the city on the ground that in full Parliament he had spoken ill of the mayor and aldermen. Even so distinguished a person as Sir John Philpot was deposed from the aldermanic bench, and Ralph Strode, the city's Common Serjeant-at-Law, was made to surrender rooms over Aldersgate which had been granted to him for life during Brembre's mayoralty.

If Northampton had been more circumspect and not offended so many powerful interests at once, he might have been successful. As it was, his position soon became precarious. To please the prudish-minded elements among the Londoners (strong it would seem among the lesser guildsmen), he conducted a campaign against sexual immorality in London and did not hesitate to trespass on the rights of the Church courts to do so. He also took action to safeguard poor people from being forced to pay more than they could afford at baptisms, marriages, and requiem masses.

In his efforts to reform the city's constitution and practices, he made it clear that he placed his confidence in the lesser guildsmen—small masters and even less important craftsmen—and not in rich merchants, even nonvictualers. Naturally this alienated the ruling class, which became increasingly alarmed at what seemed to the merchants his demagogic actions to please the lesser craftsmen. Their views were confirmed by the more radical policies of his second term of office as mayor. In the election of 1383 he was defeated by Sir Nicholas Brembre, the grocer. In reply Northampton tried to incite the lesser folk against the city authorities, and then he decided on rebellion.

On Sunday, February 7, 1384, about five hundred guildsmen were summoned to meet him at Bow Church. From there he led them through West Cheap toward Ludgate Bridge. The news was brought to Brembre as he sat at dinner with several aldermen in the house of Sir Richard Waldegrave in St. Michael Hoggenlane. They all started up and hurried after Northampton, but did not catch him until he had reached the house of the White Friars in Fleet Street. Northampton refused to disperse his followers and was arrested. He was tried before the king's council, and sent as a prisoner to Tintagel Castle in Cornwall.

Northampton appealed for help to his powerful patron John of Gaunt, but even the duke was unable to secure his pardon, for the city merchants realized that Richard resented his uncle's attempts to dominate the government and they tried to please the king by making loans to him. The king responded by supporting the suppression of Northampton and his principal supporters and by sanctioning the execution of John Constantyn, a cordwainer, who had tried to raise an insurrection in the city four days after Northampton's defiance. Richard agreed to a statute that repealed the recent act forbidding victualers to hold judicial office, and a new charter reduced merchant strangers to their former subservient position. In 1384 the right of electing the Common Council was restored to the wards, apparently because election by wards was now thought likely to favor the powerful guilds, in spite of a rule that no craft could have more than eight of its members on the council at any one time.

Brembre seems to have become unpopular in his turn. Doubtless his opponents exaggerated the charges against him, but there seems little doubt that he used force to secure his re-election in 1384. A goldsmith, Nicholas Twyford, said to be a follower of Northampton, put up for mayor against him, and Brembre is said to have defeated him only by means of armed men stationed near the Guildhall.

Brembre and the victualers continued to draw nearer to the king and their opponents began to look for support from the king's critics. In the Parliament of 1386, when the extravagance and personal government of the young king came under attack, many of the nonvictualing guilds were encouraged to make complaints against Brembre. There were petitions from the drapers, mercers, cordwainers, cutlers, saddlers, embroiderers, founders, armorers, leathersellers, painters, and pinners complaining not only that he had used force in the election of 1384, but that he had imprisoned and conspired in the death of various men without due process of law. After Richard's spirited reply to his critics in this Parliament, Brembre threw in his lot more decidedly with the king.

Brembre was mayor from October, 1383, until October, 1386, when he was succeeded by Nicholas Exton, fishmonger (who soon publicly burned the Jubilee Book outside the Guildhall). Brembre now took a greater part in national politics. He is said to have attended the famous council at Nottingham, when the king asked the judges about the legality of the proceedings of the recent Parliament. The judges' declaration in favor of the king so angered the king's opponents that civil war was clearly imminent. Instigated by Brembre, the citizens took an oath to uphold the king against all his enemies. Richard sent a gracious reply, thanking the citizens for their efforts, expressing a hope that they would choose a mayor who could be trusted to govern well and charging the city authorities not to show any favor to John of Northampton and his adherents.

The struggle soon reached a crisis. On December 1, 1387, the mayor and aldermen were summoned to Windsor where Richard asked them how many men the city could bring to his aid if necessary. In alarm, Mayor Exton replied that the citizens were not fighters, but tradesmen and craftsmen, and begged to be relieved of his office. This the king would not permit but charged him and the aldermen to keep the city safely for him. Richard then pinned his hopes on the army which his friend Robert de Vere, Duke of Ireland, was bringing from Chester. But at Radcot Bridge, on the Thames, de Vere found himself ringed by his enemies and, judging the position to be hopeless, he fled in the December fog to France. His army melted away, and Richard had no alternative but to seek refuge in the Tower of London.

The mayor and aldermen judged it politic to admit the victorious lords appellant into the city without question, to go to the Tower and make the king submit to their demand for a Parliament on their terms. When it met on February 3, Nicholas Brembre was one of the five confidants of the king who were accused of high treason. Brembre was the only one who could be arrested, as the others were in hiding or in exile. He boldly faced his accusers, and the king tried to defend him. The committee of twelve peers appointed to investigate the charges found Brembre guilty of nothing worthy of death. The indignant lords appellant therefore called on two representatives of every London guild to testify against him, but without result. This is remarkable in view of the controversies in London in the previous decade. Then the mayor and aldermen were questioned. When asked whether they thought Brembre knew of these treasonable matters, they replied cautiously that in their opinion he was more likely to have known of them than not. Then the lords questioned William Cheyne, the city recorder, who in 1386 had been regarded by the cutlers as an accomplice of Brembre. Cheyne replied with equal caution that if Brembre did know of treasonable matters and concealed his knowledge, he was doubtless worthy of death. On this flimsy evidence Brembre was then condemned to death. The case against him was so weak that the charges included indictments such as the one that he had plotted to change the name of London to New Troy.

The resentment of the appellant lords against him was, apart from a personal grudge of the Duke of Gloucester, based on indignation that a mere merchant should dare to meddle in matters of state. Perhaps, if high-spirited men like Sir William Walworth and Sir John Philpot had still been alive, they might have stirred up London on Richard's behalf. But though Exton and his fellow aldermen acted in a craven manner, they may have saved the city from repression by the appellant lords, for the divisions since the mayoralty of Northampton could have given a good excuse for interference. Exton had been close enough to the government of Richard II for the lords appellant to have taken action against him if he had not capitulated. It is significant that in October, 1388, Exton took the trouble to obtain the king's official pardon for all treasons and felonies; one of the sheriffs, William Venour, a grocer who had also served Richard, had previously done the same. To a less extent the Court of Aldermen may have feared the vengeance of the lords appellant if they did not acquiesce; for the court that deserted Brembre was almost the same in composition as the one that had written John of Gaunt in 1386 to resist the return to London of John of Northampton and had, in 1387 in a letter to Lord de la Zouche, declared their intention to stand by Richard II against his foes.

The abandonment of Brembre by his fellow aldermen, though unjust, not only saved the wealthy merchant oligarchy from attack by the appellant lords; it marked the moment when the oligarchy, realizing the grave dangers caused by its internal quarrels, decided to close ranks. In the previous decade the victualers had tried to secure their candidates as mayors in spite of opposition. Now they supported as successor to Exton a goldsmith, Nicholas Twyford, who had quarreled with Brembre in 1378 and tried to succeed him in 1384. Twyford, for his part, showed his desire to conciliate the oligarchy by making a new ordinance which gave the choice of the common councillors to the mayor, acting in the presence of at least twelve aldermen. Another ordinance, passed at the same meeting of the Court of Aldermen, laid down that no one was to remain mayor for more than a year at a time, thus giving a chance for the office to be held by more aldermen. Subsequent elections were not entirely harmonious, but the relationships amongst the merchant class were much improved. Whereas, since the accession of Richard II, the office of mayor had (except for the interlude of Northampton's regime) been dominated by victualers, for the rest of the reign there were four victualer mayors and eight nonvictualers.

Since the most recent enemy of the city had been the lords appellant, greater unity among the city's merchants should have given Richard his chance to gain renewed support from the city government. As it happened, he forfeited all support in London by his rash and haughty behavior toward the city in May, 1392, when he dismissed from office the mayor and sheriffs and sent them to prison, appointing as warden of the city his own nominee, Sir Edward Dallingridge (or Dalyngrigge), of Bodiam

Castle, Sussex, one of his household knights. The king and his council sentenced the former mayor and sheriffs to remain in prison until they had paid fine and ransom at the king's pleasure. Dallingridge was replaced as warden by Sir Baldwin Raddington, controller of the royal household and a strict disciplinarian.

Why the king took such drastic action is not clear. The city records naturally make no mention of the reasons and the chroniclers give differing accounts. One report, which survived in London tradition down to the sixteenth century, said that the king's anger was aroused by a riot of Londoners against the servant of one of his ministers. According to this tale, a baker's man was delivering bread to customers in Fleet Street. A servant of the Bishop of Salisbury, the Treasurer of England, took a loaf from the basket of bread and struck the man with a dagger when he tried to snatch it back. The neighbors then tried to arrest the servant for a breach of the peace, but his fellow servants streamed out of the bishop's house and rescued him. A crowd then gathered and tried to break into the house to lay hold of the servant. This may be true, for such fights between haughty servants of great lords and Londoners often occurred. (In 1321 an esquire of the Earl of Arundel, riding through Thames Street on his way to the Tower, nearly knocked down a woman carrying a child. When a passerby bade him ride with more care, the squire cut him down with his sword.)

But the reason given by most contemporary sources for the king's drastic action was that he had been very short of money and had been angered by the Londoners' reluctance to lend it. According to fuller versions of this story, the king was especially angry because, having failed to get the loan for which he had asked the city, he obtained it from a Lombard who had borrowed it with ease from the very Londoners who had told the king that they were too impoverished to lend to him. The king thereupon decided to punish the city by removing the law courts to York (thus depriving the Londoners of the employment brought by their presence) and by taking the city government into his hand, in spite of a statute of 1354 saying that this was to be only for a third offense. Not only were the law courts sent to York but also the Exchequer and the Chancery in spite of the hardships caused to the clients and staffs of the courts. The former mayor and sheriffs were fined 3,000 marks and London was ordered to pay an enormous fine of £100,000.

Thanks either to the queen's intercession, as the chroniclers said, or the fading away of the king's wrath, this harsh treatment did not last long. In August the city prepared a fine pageant for the king and queen, ending with the presentation to them at Westminster of £10,000. This did the trick. On September 19, 1392, the fines imposed on the city, the mayor, and sheriffs were remitted; the latter were released from prison, and the city was fully restored to the king's favor. The courts were told to return from York, and in October, 1392, the keeper of the city was replaced by a newly elected mayor, William Staundon, a grocer. Outwardly the relations between king and city seemed to be entirely restored to harmony, and in 1395 the city government endorsed the loyal good wishes of the Commons in Parliament when Richard crossed to Ireland.

But in reality the Londoners never forgot the humiliations of 1392. Their resentments were increased by the king's actions during the last two years of his reign. After the Parliament of Shrewsbury, with the condemnation of Gloucester, Arundel, and Warwick and the banishment of Bolingbroke and Mowbray, Richard thought himself secure and able to wreak vengeance for the events of 1388. The Londoners, who had already learned how vengeful the king could be, presented a petition couched in very lowly terms, acknowledging that they had grievously offended him and deserved heavy chastisement, praying him to be merciful, and promising to be utterly faithful lieges in future. The king, in reply, caused many blank charters to be made and told the members of the various crafts of London to come to the Guildhall to set their seals to these charters, which rendered them liable to provide Richard with whatever sums of money he chose to exact from them. According to a London chronicle written in 1443, giving a detailed version of the events of these years, Richard got his way with London by sending his Cheshire soldiers into the city one night, which led to a great clash with the Londoners.

Richard may have realized the need to make some friends in London at this time. At any rate, just before he set off for Ireland he restored all the privileges of the London fishmongers. He proclaimed by letters patent that no foreigner was to be allowed to sell fish retail in the city, that no foreigner was to sell fish to another foreigner within the city for resale, that all fish coming by water was to be landed during daylight between Billingsgate and Queenhithe, and that all fresh fish was to be sold at Bridge Street, Old Fish Street, or the Stocks. Moreover, he restored to the fishmongers the privilege they had lost by statute in 1382, during the mayoralty of Northampton, that of holding their own "halimot," or court, to regulate the trade in fish, thus giving them the power to raise the price of this essential commodity if they wished.

This action shows Richard's ineptitude. It was intensely unpopular (except among the fishmongers), for it aroused memories of all the bitter strife of past years. The result was that when Henry of Lancaster invaded the country and swept all before him, the Londoners accepted his victory with alacrity. So hated was the fallen king that Henry sent him secretly by water from Westminster to the Tower of London. Nevertheless the news spread and a great crowd of Londoners gathered to intercept Richard, presumably at the entrance to the Tower, "and so to have slayn hym for the great crueltie that he before tyme hadde used unto the citie." The mayor and sheriffs heard of this and gathered a force of more responsible Londoners to prevent violence, but they had great difficulty in turning away the hostile crowd. Balked of their prey, the throng marched to Westminster, seized the unfortunate Nicholas Slake, dean of the king's chapel, brought him to Newgate prison, and cast him in irons.

After this stormy period the government of London moved into calmer waters. Henry IV realized the need to conciliate London. Richard's letters patent to the fishmongers were revoked in Henry's first Parliament, and though Henry was glad of any money that he could get, he was very careful to treat the city merchants with respect. Henry V similarly took care to cultivate the good will of the city government, even sending special letters to the mayor and citizens to inform them of the course of his victories in France. In spite of his prestige he was always scrupulous to ask for money instead of demanding it. It is true that Henry VI lost the confidence of the Londoners, but Edward IV and Henry VII both worked hard to win it. No fifteenth-century king tried to take the government of London into his own hand as Richard had done in 1392.

Not only was the city government more free from outside interference, but it was also more stable within. The lower classes now acquiesced in the control of the merchant class; victualers and nonvictualers alike had learned from the strife of Richard II's reign that they must not carry their differences too far. This stability was reflected in the lack of controversy about the city's constitution compared with the acrimonious changes of the late fourteenth century. Changes there were in the city government in the fifteenth century, but small and smoothly achieved compared with those of Richard II's time.

For many Londoners this quieter aftermath must have been a boon. There must have been many who, like Chaucer, suffered in the violent reversal of fortune of their patrons. Owing to the influence of his patron, John of Gaunt, Chaucer was appointed in 1374 to the responsible post of controller of the wool custom and subsidy and of the petty custom in the port of London. The previous month he had, perhaps through the same influence, been granted a lease for life of a house above Aldgate, subject only to the mayor's right of entry if need should arise to defend the city from there. Drawn into the king's service, he won recognition partly by his administrative services and partly by the literary works which began to flow from his pen. In 1382 he was granted another controllership of customs in London and in 1383 he was given the right to appoint a deputy controller. Appointed a justice of the peace for Kent in 1385, he was elected a knight of the shire for that county in 1386.

But he was too much in favor with the party of Brembre in London and with the de la Pole group round the king. In the Parliament of 1386 the attacks on the government led to his loss of both controllerships and of his house in Aldgate. In 1388–89 the zeal of the lords appellant to strike alike at the king's extravagance and supporters caused Chaucer to be deprived of all his exchequer annuities. For a while he must have been reduced from affluence and importance to poverty and obscurity. It is true that in July, 1389, when the king had been able to reassert himself somewhat, Chaucer was appointed Clerk of the Works at Westminster Palace and the Tower of London and that in the 1390's this was followed by various annuities from the king. But Chaucer's sudden misfortunes in 1386 and 1388 must have left him with a feeling of insecurity. Not all victims of the political upheavals were so fortunate as he was.

The political upheavals were a misfortune for the lesser craftsmen as well. The victory of the merchants against John of Northampton's attempts to champion the interests of lesser men meant that economic forces were able to develop unchecked. As the commercial and industrial importance of London continued to grow, the number of craft guilds increased. Some of the humbler crafts were not organized into guilds, as we can see from the list of 111 crafts compiled by the Brewers' clerk in 1422, but all the wealthier crafts aspired to have a proper guild.

As already explained, it became the ambition of the stronger guilds to safeguard their position by obtaining a royal charter, but this cost a good deal of money to obtain and the guilds which were, on the whole, in the best position to make money were the trading guilds, not the wholly or predominantly craft guilds. The latter had to be content with sanction from the mayor, who scrutinized their ordinances, allowed or disallowed them, and acted as judge in any dispute between their members or between the guild and an outsider. In the Parliament of 1389, when there was much concern about the maintenance of order and the prevention of conspiracy among the lower classes, a royal inquiry into the rules of guilds was instituted. Criticism was expressed in Parliament of the use of livery or special uniform by some guilds, of the economic power they could gain by holding lands, and of the secrecy of their proceedings. The inquiry revealed that the guild form of organization was very strong in London. Not only were there nearly a hundred craft guilds in existence, but almost as many parish fraternities, clubs associated with parish churches, admitting usually both men and women as members and existing primarily to provide masses for the welfare of the souls of their members and kinsmen. Many of these parish fraternities were able to protest, like the wardens of the Guild of St. Bride, Fleet Street, that they had no lands, held no secret assemblies, and attached no significance to their livery. Such protestations made the craft guilds seem vulnerable, for they either held or wished to hold lands and secret meetings and wanted a livery with a significant meaning. Clearly the best way to safeguard their position was to obtain, if they could afford it, a royal charter which none would dare to question.

Therefore, in 1390, the Taylors led the way by securing a charter which confirmed their right to hold assemblies and an annual feast at midsummer, to make ordinances, to wear a livery. The charters granted to the Goldsmiths and Mercers in 1394 and the Saddlers in 1395 go much further. Each of these crafts obtained the right to have a perpetual community of themselves, i.e., to be incorporated and to have the right to hold lands corporately to the value of £20. Once this occurred, it became the ambition of all the greater guilds to be incorporated and in the reign of Henry VI nine of them succeeded: the Grocers, Fishmongers, Vintners, Brewers, Drapers, Cordwainers, Leathersellers, Haberdashers, and Armorers, preceded by the Cutlers in the previous reign.

The fifteenth century thus saw the working out of tendencies which were already apparent in Chaucer's day. The great trading companies fortified their position by royal charters and drew apart from the lesser companies, at first only in social esteem, but by the early sixteenth century in formal precedence, in official privilege (such as participating in the election of the mayor), and social consequence (such as enrolling the king among their membership and attending the mayor at coronations). Many of the craft guilds fell under the domination of the trading guilds, which in some cases actually absorbed them. Thus the Leathersellers first claimed rights of search of craftsmen working in leather, to ensure good standards of workmanship, as they said, and eventually absorbed the Tawyers, Pursers, Glovers, and Pouchmakers. The Armorers took control of the Bladesmiths and Brasiers. The Hatters and Cappers fell under the domination of the Haberdashers. The amalgamation of the Fullers and Shearmen made a guild strong enough to secure last place among the Twelve Great Companies, but it was the only partially craft guild in this select band and the other eleven—Mercers, Grocers, Drapers, Fishmongers, Goldsmiths, Skinners, Taylors, Haberdashers, Salters, Ironmongers, and Vintners—were predominantly or wholly trading companies.

In these great companies a tendency already apparent in the fourteenth century became more pronounced in the fifteenth. The traders who bought and sold wholesale were usually in a better position to make bigger profits and to grow wealthy than those who bought and sold retail. The wholesalers regarded themselves as socially superior and began to draw apart from the retailers. In the fourteenth century the cost of entry into the guild was a modest sum and theoretically the same for all, though it was already greater in the more affluent guilds than in the lesser ones. For example, the fee for binding an apprentice was normally 2s in the wealthy guild of mercers, but 1s in the humbler guild of carpenters; and at the end of an apprentice's term a mercer had to pay 20s on admission to the guild whereas a carpenter paid only 3s/4d. A common figure for the annual subscription of a master craftsman was 1s a year, paid in quarterly installments known as "quarterage."

But already in the fourteenth century a distinction was appearing in many crafts between the ordinary members of the craft and a select band who took the lead in the guild. In an age which believed in having outward forms to express economic and social realities, this distinction was symbolized by a special dress. At a meeting of a select group of grocers in 1345 the wearing of a livery was prescribed, and the precise nature of this was defined in the grocers' ordinances of 1348. What was termed the "full suit" was to consist of a coat and surcote, together with a cloak and hood reserved for ceremonial occasions. The livery was usually in two bright colors, chosen by the wardens. Violet and crimson, violet and scarlet, and blue and gold were some of the colors selected as pairs. There was soon to be a part dress form, called "the hooding," or head cover, which was allowed to brethren not considered to belong to "the full livery." This livery was to be worn by a fraternity of twenty-one men, soon to be known as the Fraternity of St. Anthony, who agreed in 1345 to meet regularly and to hire a priest to pray for their souls, each paying 1d a week for his support.

Some guilds already had larger fraternities, perhaps because longer established. The Skinners, for example, had in the 1340's a Fraternity of Corpus Christi which consisted of at least fifty and probably of about seventy people. Like other fraternities within the guilds, this society had a religious purpose. In 1393 the appointment of two chaplains was described as customary from days of old, and like other fraternities it was a kind of exclusive club within the craft, including among its ranks the "top people" of the trade as well as other distinguished persons. The Skinners' Fraternity of Corpus Christi, for example, enjoyed the patronage of Edward III and Queen Philippa, the Black Prince, Richard II and Queen Anne, and enrolled among its members noblemen and great merchants like Sir John Philpot, even though he was a grocer by trade.

At first these fraternities were informal bodies, exercising authority within the guild in an important but unofficial way. Then came the royal inquiry of 1389 which cast doubt on the legality of guilds and the wearing of liveries. So the leading guilds started to obtain charters to put their legal status beyond doubt, and in these charters they obtained legal recognition of their ruling fraternity. Thus the charter of 1390 to the Merchant Taylors named the Fraternity of St. John the Baptist; the charter of 1393 to the Skinners gave royal recognition to the Fraternity of Corpus Christi; in 1378–79 the Weavers founded a fraternity in honor of the Assumption of the Virgin; and so on.

By the end of the century the leading guilds were turning into livery companies, dominated by a fraternity to which only the leading men of the trade could belong. This fraternity imposed special burdens on those who wished to be admitted: a special entrance fee, a special subscription, an expensive livery which was changed every two years, and the obligation to subscribe for special purposes. Soon the special purposes would include not only subscriptions for religious objects, such as the stipend of a priest or the provision of masses, but the building of a hall, which served, not only as a valuable social center, but as the outward sign of the dignity of the craft and its ruling society. Moreover, it was a building for the administration of the laws of the guild, a center for dispensing charity to guild members, and an office for supervising the guild estates and collecting the rents.

The early fifteenth century was a great time for the building of such halls, for the greater companies now had the wealth to do it, the ruling societies had reached a stage of recognition and dignity where they wished to acquire a visible status of this kind, and once one company had planned to build a hall, its rivals hastened to catch up by also building a hall. In the reign of Richard II only two crafts are known for certain to have possessed halls, the Taylors and the Goldsmiths; by the reign of Richard III there were twenty-eight halls of city companies and others were in course of being built. As George Unwin said: "such a mansion was almost an exact replica of the house of a great noble. . . . Indeed, many of the wealthier companies began by taking over the mansion of a feudal magnate, or the buildings of a religious community."

In 1331 the Merchant Taylors acquired a hall in Threadneedle Street which had until then been occupied by Sir Oliver Ingham. In the fifteenth century they spent such large sums on it that the banqueting hall held two hundred guests and was splendid enough, with its Flemish glass, its tapestries, and its gilded image of St. John the Baptist, to entertain the royal members of the fraternity. The Goldsmiths acquired the site of their hall in 1357 in Foster Lane from Sir Nicholas de Segrave, brother of the Bishop of London. In 1365 they spent £136 on building a hall, kitchen, pantry, buttery, and two chambers, and in 1380 they added a wainscotted parlor and a cellar. In the next century the parlor was rebuilt. The hall was beautified with a bay window, and a lantern and vane. It was hung with red worsted, paved with tiles, furnished with five benches of tapestry work with goldsmiths' arms and seven cushions to match, and adorned with a silver-gilt image of St. Dunstan (patron saint of the Goldsmith's fraternity) above the screen. Some of the later halls were even more splendid; the Grocers provided theirs with a garden and vineyard for the liverymen to enjoy. But these halls, like the other amenities of the company, cost a good deal of money, and the liverymen were expected to contribute large sums for the company's needs when the call came.

The burdens of the liverymen were therefore notable even in Chaucer's day, and in the next century they were to become even heavier. But there was compensation in the assured position of the liverymen in the guild and in the city government. Only the liverymen took part in the election of the officials of the guild, the master and wardens who met together regularly in a customary place (the company's hall, as soon as it was built) to consider breaches of the ordinances, to arbitrate in disputes between members, to sanction new apprentices, to admit new members, and to discuss with liverymen matters affecting the prosperity and reputation of the trade. Only liverymen could hope to be elected to these offices, to savor the pride of having the cap of maintenance, a headband of velvet and ermine, placed on their brows by the retiring officers. Only liverymen had the satisfaction of leading the fraternity in procession on public occasions, clad in splendid livery, and of presiding over guild feasts which might include distinguished honorary liverymen, such as members of the royal family or the nobility. Only liverymen had the right to share in the annual elections for the mayor and sheriffs, to hope to become aldermen themselves, and perhaps eventually to be sheriff or mayor.

Town dwellers in Chaucer's time were strongly gregarious, and there had to be some form of society for those lesser masters of the guild who were shut out of the livery company. These lesser men might find some consolation in joining a parish fraternity, with its chantry chaplain, its altar in the parish church, its common attendance at the funerals and anniversary masses of its members, its subscriptions, its sickness and funeral benefits, and its annual feast on the day of the patronal festival. In the late fourteenth century there were many of these fraternities in London and most of them had a large and active membership. But for the lesser freemen, or yeomen as they were called, of a large and prosperous craft guild, another prospect of community organization often unfolded in Chaucer's day: a guild fraternity which was to some extent a copy of the fraternity of the liverymen.

For example, when the Fraternity of Corpus Christi was consolidating its hold over the Skinners Company in the reign of Richard II, another fraternity was forming for the yeomen skinners. By the 1390's this yeomen's club was known as the Fraternity of Our Lady's Assumption and was attached to the church of St. John Walbrook. It obviously could not aspire to rule the company and its activities were more akin to those of a parish fraternity—masses for the souls of members, relief of the sick and poor, annual dinners, etc.—but it evidently met such a need that its membership was large and it attracted many gifts. By the middle of the fifteenth century it had a considerable store of plate, linen, and ecclesiastical vestments and its four wardens were carrying forward balances at the year end of nearly £100. By that time it had a considerable honorary membership—men from other guilds, Hanseatic merchants and Lombards, merchants from other towns, gentry, lawyers, and parsons—and it attracted the patronage of the queens of both Henry VI and Edward IV.

The story of these yeomen guilds is a useful reminder to us that in a hierarchical society it is not only the men at the top who may have an honored position in society. The dignity of the yeomen guilds (many of which evolved their own livery and rules for the wearing of it) probably contributed powerfully to the contentment of the yeomen masters and hence to the stability of London society. If yeomen craftsmen were tempted to look up in envy at the privileges of the liverymen, they could look down with condescension at the lowlier position of the journeymen of their guild, mere employees who were not members of the guild or freemen and probably never would be. Still more precarious was the position of the "foreign" craftsmen, men who were usually too poor to pay the fees of either city or guild and therefore had no recognized position in the city at all.

The authorities who took action against "foreigners" (that is, nonfreemen Englishmen as well as aliens) might well be the master and wardens of the craft, concerned as they always were to maintain the monopoly rights of the guild over that trade in London, but it might also be the mayor and aldermen. They were responsible to the king for the good government and order of the city and this could cover a wide range of matters. It meant that anyone who alleged some trade or craft malpractice could, if he wished, complain directly to the city authorities instead of to the master and wardens of the appropriate guild. In 1381, for example, a clerk ordered a gown from a skinner, but found when the gown was delivered that what purported to be a robe of new beaver skins contained a number of old otter skins. Enraged, the clerk did not appeal to the master and wardens of the Skinners Company, although it had made an ordinance in 1365 forbidding just this kind of trick. He went straight to the mayor and aldermen and charged John Donyngton with the offense. The accused made no defense and was committed to Newgate for fourteen days. When released he had to pay 13s/4d to the city chamberlain (that is, city treasurer) and 6s/8d to the guild.

It will be noted that the mayor and aldermen took judicial action and did not refer the matter to some separate judicial officer. This illustrates one of the differences between the fourteenth-century Mayor of London (and its present Lord Mayor) and the usual English mayor of our time. The Mayor of London was by virtue of his office much concerned in the administration of justice in the city. Not only was he usually a justice of the peace toward the end of the century, but there was a range of city courts in which he was involved.

The oldest of these was the Court of Husting, held at the west end of the Guildhall and presided over by the mayor or the sheriffs. It must have made a heavy demand on the mayor's time, for it met every Monday and continued on Tuesday if its business could not be concluded in one day. It transacted both administrative and legal business; deeds, wills, and indentures were enrolled there and the court heard action by writ dealing with land and tenements, suits about rents or services, and disputes about wills. It was busy with the unusual privilege of enrollment and probate of wills.[1]

---

[1] Normally jurisdiction over wills was the prerogative of the Church courts and in theory wills could normally deal only with personal property. But jurisdiction over wills was claimed by the city as

The Court of Husting was, indeed, so busy that the Sheriffs' Court had already started as an overflow and had developed into a flourishing court which, along with the Mayor's Court, was eventually to supersede the Husting Court. This was partly because the Sheriffs' Court was dealing with classes of cases which were expanding rapidly, such as disputes between merchants ranging from debt to claims of account or seizure of goods, to be settled by the law merchant. It was also partly because the procedure was more flexible, admitting more easily action by petition and using newer forms such as trespass. It made, however, much use of oath-helping, or compurgation; that is, if there were no authentic documents in a case of debt, for instance, the defendant could try to clear himself with the aid of the oath of six Londoners of repute. If he were an outsider, he could try to find two men of repute to be his oath-helpers. If he failed to find two oath-helpers, the defendant was to go with the serjeant of the court to the six churches nearest to the Guildhall and swear his innocence on the Blessed Sacrament in each of them.

If the mayor thought fit, he could remove a case from the Sheriffs' Court to the Mayor's Court, which could hear as a court of first instance many of the actions received by the Sheriffs' Court, with which it therefore competed. In addition, it especially considered cases of theft, brawling, rioting, swindling, and any disobedience to the

early as 1230 and made good in a dispute with the Bishop of London in 1268. London citizens could openly bequeath both real and personal property, subject to the widow's right of dower. In such a busy commercial center there was naturally a great deal of enrolling of wills and deeds.

city's ordinances. The Mayor's Court was so important that in 1377 its serjeants successfully petitioned for the provision of liveries or uniforms; the dignity of the city must be upheld when they proclaimed and enforced the ordinances of the mayor and Common Council. The chief of these serjeants was the Common Serjeant, who acted as a public prosecutor for the court. He had a special responsibility to prosecute on behalf of city orphans brought to his attention where the guardian was guilty of wasting the ward's property, or of ill-treatment, or of forcing them into marriage.

So important had this court become by the middle of the fourteenth century that it was too much for the mayor to preside as a matter of routine. The normal president of the court was the recorder, a professional lawyer trained in an inn of court, who acted as general legal adviser to the mayor and aldermen and on many occasions as the voice of the city, e.g., in reading an address of welcome to visiting princes. But the mayor could and did still act in many ways as head of the Mayor's Court or outer chamber. He could, for example, take action to protect apprentices, as he did in 1398 when he ordered the hurers, makers of rough caps, not to send their apprentices down to the Thames and other exposed places in tempests, frosts, or snows. He also disciplined apprentices, if requested, and arranged for difficult cases of transfer or default of apprenticeship. As the rendering of account often entered into the matter, he developed the habit of associating the chamberlain of the city with him in apprenticeship cases. This habit laid the foundations of the

Chamberlain's Court which had fully developed by the sixteenth century to deal with questions of apprenticeship.

The administration of justice was by no means the only duty of the mayor, who had much more independent power and responsibility than the average modern English mayor. The latter is the chairman of a body on which power is conferred by statute and the decisions are those of the council, not of the chairman. But the Mayor of London in Chaucer's day had a wide regulating power on his own authority, as well as the function of issuing precepts on behalf of the Crown without reference to aldermen or Common Council. He claimed the right to revise the ordinances of the guilds and in case of dispute between rival companies the final decision lay with him. He had, moreover, much more executive authority than the modern English mayor. From 1396, for example, he was responsible for regulating the sale of cloth at the newly acquired Blackwell (or Bakewell) Hall, near the Guildhall.

Along with the sheriffs he was responsible for the maintenance of order in London and he was expected to take the initiative if any breach of the peace seemed imminent. So prominent was the mayor in this vital duty that he was likely to be severely blamed if any disorder occurred. When in 1471 it became clear that there might be trouble because of the impending invasion by Edward IV, the mayor, John Stockton, thought it prudent to feign sickness and keep to his bed.

London was important enough to have a number of civic officials, such as the chamberlain for financial matters, the common clerk for secretarial functions, the recorder and common sergeants for judicial work. But whenever important decisions had to be made or discretion used, these officials looked to the mayor. He was expected to maintain a large household, with a number of leading officials—the swordbearer, the common hunt, the common crier, the water bailiff, the serjeant-at-arms, serjeants of the chamber and serjeants of the mayor—not to speak of a large staff of lesser officials, from yeomen downward. The mayor was responsible for the reception and entertainment of official guests and was expected to do this, at the city's expense, in a style worthy of so great a city. Thus in January, 1308, when Queen Isabella wrote from Windsor to the mayor and aldermen and commonalty of London to tell them of the birth of her son, the future Edward III, the mayor invited her to a sumptuous feast at the Guildhall. Another splendid banquet took place there in May, 1357, when the mayor and aldermen entertained Edward, the Black Prince, and his captive, King John of France.

The Guildhall in which these and other feasts were held was not the one gutted by fire in 1940. That was begun in 1411, and successive mayors put great efforts into the building of it until Richard Whittington's executors came to their help in the 1420's with fine glass for the windows and splendid tiles for the floor. Evidently the previous Guildhall was not good enough for London's pride, though it had been enlarged in 1326 and extensively repaired in 1341–43. Standing just to the north of St. Lawrence Jewry's churchyard, the old Guildhall was fairly extensive by the reign of Richard II. It had a great hall with an upper chamber over it, an inner chamber where courts were held, a cellar, an outer and a middle gate, two gardens, and a chapel served by five priests. But evidently it was not an impressive building and the mayor was, by contrast, becoming very grand.

His entry into office was marked by splendid ceremonies and at coronations he carried the city scepter. In 1379 he was assessed for the poll tax as an earl. In 1415, when the archbishops and the king's brothers were to be received at the Guildhall, it was decided that because it was in the city, the mayor should take precedence over all and sit in the middle. Indeed by that time Londoners had come to claim that in the city the mayor should take precedence over everyone except the king, and they were ready to support any mayor who enforced this claim. In 1464 the mayor was invited to the royal feast in honor of the serjeants-at-law. It was held at Ely Place, the London house of the Bishop of Ely, which was within the liberties of the city. It seemed to the mayor essential to claim precedence in his own city; so when he arrived and found that the Treasurer of England, Lord Grey of Ruthin, was already seated in the place which he thought ought to be his, he left at once, with the aldermen, and ordered a meal at his own house. At short notice he managed to produce such a fine dinner, complete with cygnets and other delicacies, that when the officers of the serjeants' feast, to make amends, sent presents of meat, bread, wine, and sugar confections, the servants were ashamed to present them. The mayor thanked the messengers graciously and gave them a reward. The city won handsomely in this contest of prestige. One chronicler's comment was: "And so the worship of the city was kept and not lost for him and I trust that it never shall be, by the grace of God." The late Stephen Potter had a word for it: Oneupmanship.

Also conscious of their dignity were the sheriffs and aldermen of the city. The sheriffs, two in number—"the mayor's eyes," as Stow called them—were sheriffs of Middlesex as well as the city. After 1347, one was nominated by the mayor, the other (after 1384) elected by the Common Council assisted by the masters and wardens of the guilds and honest men of their liveries. The sheriffs were the police officers of the city who arrested offenders and lodged them in prison to await the next jail delivery. They could hold preliminary inquests with a jury from a ward in which an offense had been committed and present a suspect to the justices sitting in the Tower. The sheriffs were responsible for the court that bore their name. They worked hard for its success and tried to secure for it the sole right of hearing actions of debt, for they needed the fees and fines that it brought in to help to recoup them for the £300 they had to pay into the Exchequer each year for their shrievalty.

The sheriffs were chosen from the aldermen, who were until 1394 elected annually by the wards; thereafter they were appointed for life. This tended to make the body of aldermen an exclusive group, and this trend was powerfully increased by an ordinance of 1397 which provided that the mayor and existing aldermen could, in an aldermanic vacancy, choose one of two candidates to be put up by the ward. In 1402 the scales were further tipped in favor of the mayor and existing aldermen, who could henceforth choose from four candidates; this remained the law until 1711. These changes favored the predominance of the great trading guilds, and in the fifteenth century it became the rule that aldermen should always be members of the twelve great livery companies. If they were not members at the time of their election, they were admitted to one.

The aldermen were especially responsible for the good government of their wards (twenty-five in number after the division of Farringdon Ward in 1393). They saw that the male population of their ward was assessed to arms; they set the watch and levied the trained bands of their wards; they kept the peace and the gates of the city; they were responsible for the highways and waterways of their wards; they tried weights and measures; and they presided over the wardmoots. Increasingly they were made justices of the peace and fixed wages for journeymen and apprentices. They were closely associated with the mayor as advisers, as formal presidents with him of the Mayor's Court, and as fellow members of the Inner Chamber, which prepared ordinances to lay before the Common Council and could veto measures passed there.

The Court of Common Council was not only subject to this constitutional check, but to an informal one as well. Not only were the mayor and aldermen members of the Common Council, but in spite of the ordinance of 1384, which gave the election of the commoners to the wards, the aldermen often exercised much influence over the choice of common councilmen. Nevertheless, it was to be of importance in the future that the common councilmen were elected. Together with the fact that the charters of 1341, 1377, and 1383 gave to the mayor, aldermen, and common councilors the power to amend the constitution, their election meant that the city of London possessed the power of self-reform and saved it, alone of the old corporations, from the revolution of the Municipal Corporations Reform Act of 1835. Even in Chaucer's day the Council already had a role of some importance, for it shared in the administration of London, confirmed the issue of ordinances by the mayor, and controlled the estates of the city.

In addition to the many courts and officials who exercised authority over the whole city, there were now officials for special areas of it. There was, for example, the bailiff of Southwark, appointed by the city after 1327. In that year young Edward III granted to London the bailiwick of Southwark for a rent of £10 a year, because the citizens had complained that thieves, felons, and other malefactors were escaping from London into Southwark where they could not be pursued by the city's officials. Edward's charter enabled the Londoners, through their bailiff, to make arrests in Southwark, hold courts there, and levy fines and tolls. Until 1462, however, there remained considerable doubt about the extent of London's rights in Southwark, in relation to those of the sheriff of Surrey and the Bishop of Winchester, and this gave room for the persistence of disorder there. Moreover, the bailiff of Southwark did not always please the Londoners. When John of Northampton was mayor and was campaigning against the power of the city victualers, he accused the bailiff of Southwark, then a fishmonger, of detaining fish belonging to strangers so that it arrived too late for the market. The bailiff was dismissed and it was decreed that in future fish for the city coming from the south should not be unloaded in Southwark but should be taken straight through to Cornhill, the Stocks Market, and West Cheap.

Other officials with responsibility for a particular area were the wardens of London Bridge. The city had been entrusted with the care of the bridge even before the erection of Peter of Colechurch's stone bridge between 1176 and 1209. To pay for this, Henry II helped by granting a tax on wool, and his son John allowed the rents and profits of houses to be built on the bridge to be devoted to its repair and maintenance. Henry III, however, seized the revenues of the bridge for long periods between 1249 and 1272. The result was that in 1280 Edward I had to issue an appeal for funds and stated that the bridge was so ruinous it was in danger of collapse. He therefore allowed the mayor and citizens to levy tolls on every man and horsepack crossing the bridge. This royal patronage encouraged many private benefactions by persons of all ranks, down to William King, laborer, who bequeathed 10s for its upkeep.

One valuable source of revenue was the land on which the Stocks Market was held. By Chaucer's day the bridge was well endowed and the management of its revenues from lands, tenements, rents, tolls, and commodities was a considerable responsibility.

Major decisions were in the hands of the Common Council, but for small matters and for the twice yearly audit of accounts there was a committee of two aldermen and four commoners elected annually. The accounts and the management of the bridge were in the hands of two wardens chosen each year. The earliest surviving accounts are those of 1382 and from these "bridge-masters accounts" we learn that the wardens were paid a salary of £10 a year each. This was quite substantial, especially as there were considerable perquisites. By 1468 we find the auditors trying to curb extravagance by ordering that the wardens, or bridge-masters, were not to keep horses on the grounds of the business of the bridge, but to hire them if necessary.

The wardens probably earned their salaries, however, for there was much to be done. They not only had to account for all the diverse revenues but to pursue in court, before the mayor and aldermen, tenants who did not pay their rent. In a rental prepared by the wardens in 1358, the bridge property is described as situated in London, Southwark, Hatcham, Camberwell, Lewisham, and Stratford-le-Bow. On the bridge alone there were 138 shops with a rent roll of £160/4/od. The wardens had to look after not only the bridge, but any other property that was part of the trust. For example, the stocks in the Stocks Market had to be washed and colored when important royal visitors were expected. The Market was rebuilt in 1410–11.

The large Bridge House, with its own wharf, stood at the south end of London Bridge from the thirteenth century. From there the wardens supervised a large staff, to whom were paid out not only wages and Christmas boxes while they worked, but pensions when they retired. They were assisted by executive officers such as the accountant, the renter, and the clerk of the works. In the earliest wardens' account we find them supervising a clerk of the drawbridge, six carpenters, four masons, two sawyers, one sailor (perhaps to collect tolls from ships passing under the bridge), a cook and keeper of the dogs, a carter and horses, a boy, a paviour, a plasterer and his servant, and twenty-one tidesmen working at the ram (for pile driving) for six hours. Other workmen—plumbers, plasterers, tilers, painters, and smiths—were employed as need arose.

Soon extra men and materials had to be paid for, since in 1384 another chapel was started on the bridge. Peter of Colechurch, designer of the bridge, had provided a chapel, dedicated to St. Thomas, in the middle of the bridge, but so many endowed chantries had been provided for it afterward that between 1384 and 1397 the bridge-wardens added an upper chapel. The Perpendicular Gothic style in which it was designed naturally meant a number of large windows and the provision of glass was a heavy expense. The accounts for 1397 show the purchase of 106½ feet of white glass and 150 feet of stained glass containing images and shields. The wardens also paid the clerk of the chapel and four chaplains. On July 7, the feast of the Translation of St. Thomas, and on Christmas Day there were payments to singers for full choral services. These services would be the more impressive by reason of the costly vestments, the silver-gilt plate, and the finely-bound service books with which the chapel had already been endowed and for which the wardens were responsible.

A different kind of payment was made to boatmen, especially to the "shouteman" in charge of the large barge, or "shoute," that brought materials for the repair of the bridge. Owing to the heavy traffic always thronging over the bridge and the impact of the tides on the nineteen massive piers obstructing the flow of water (not to mention the jousts sometimes held on the bridge), repairs were incessant. Indeed, the condition of the bridge gave cause for anxiety from time to time. In 1424–25 one of the middle arches was inspected and found cracked and "the watercourse of the Thames was seen below." In alarm the mayor and aldermen made an ordinance forbidding anyone to drive over the bridge any carriage shod with iron on pain of imprisonment and a fine of 6s/8d. Crises continued to occur and in 1498 the repairs to the drawbridge were so urgent that 18d was given to the workmen as a reward "to forbear their luncheons [or tea-breaks as we might say] and sleep for the greater speed of the work."

The hard work of the bridge-wardens was not without its rewards, however. The accounts record the payments for feeding the "game" of swans which the wardens kept on the Thames. There were also the feasts. Each year there was a breakfast to celebrate the "swann-upping" and another annual feast was held at Bridge House when the

mayor, aldermen, and recorder came to view the stores
and receive the audited accounts. An extra feast could
always be justified if the mayor was called upon to view
dilapidations, obstructions, and encroachments. And the
lively Southwark fair, which extended its stalls to the
bridge, was held each year on September 7, 8, and 9. As
the route over the bridge between the houses and shops
was already very narrow, it is not clear where room was
found for stalls, unless it was at the three openings, one
of which was the drawbridge. What is certain is that it
was a perfect excuse for a visit of inspection by the mayor,
sheriffs, and aldermen, all in their gorgeous liveries,
riding in procession to St. Magnus Church at the north
end of the bridge, then over the bridge to the fair and
back to Bridge House, where a banquet was held.

Naturally Bridge House had to be worthy of so important a visitor as the Mayor of London, especially as it
was also used for sessions and other city business connected
with Southwark. Hence from Chaucer's time onward the
bridge accounts show expenditure to make the chambers
used by the mayor and aldermen more attractive: money
for glass with coats of arms, for hangings of red say, for a
green carpet, for mural decorations, and so on. By the
fifteenth century the Bridge House had a fine garden,
with an arbor, fountains, and ponds, which formed an
additional attraction for the annual audit feast.

Numerous as were the officials appointed by the city,
they were not the only people concerned with the government of London. Both the king and the Church had a
say in the matter. Admittedly by Chaucer's time the king's

interventions were very limited compared with the extensive royal justice normally administered elsewhere within the realm. An "iter" was held by the king's justices at the Tower of London at long intervals, sometimes as much as twenty years. The king's justice inquired into all cases of unnatural death since their last visit and into all cases of felony awaiting trial.

Since the visit had a strong money-making aspect, all the city officials involved—aldermen, sheriffs, witnesses, and jurors—were liable to fines for any mistake, great or small, in the presentation of the cases or in the procedure they had followed at the time of the death, perhaps years before. Even the prisoners were subjected to these financial pressures, for if they were convicted of felony, the Crown got all their chattels. According to common law, a defendant could not be tried unless he consented to a trial by jury. With the fate of hanging and confiscation before him, a guilty person might be tempted to refuse to plead. To prevent this such a prisoner was shut up in Newgate in a bare cell, with not even a truss of straw to lie on and barely enough bread and water to keep him alive. The fourteenth-century coroners' rolls, although incomplete, record several instances of prisoners who died in Newgate from this kind of treatment. Newgate, the prison for felons, had a reputation for harsh treatment and jail fever. Stow tells how in the middle of the fifteenth century the prisoners revolted and took to the roof of the gate, from which they defied the sheriffs for several hours. By comparison, Ludgate and Fleet prisons, used primarily for debtors, were comparatively humane and tolerable, unsanitary though they were.

Almost as much disliked by Londoners as the court at the Tower was the court held by the king's justices from time to time at the church of St. Martin-le-Grand. Patronized by the Norman kings, it was already a royal free chapel in the twelfth century and by the thirteenth century it was free from all authority except that of the king. It was governed by a college of deans and canons, who were usually absentees in the king's service; hence the king usually backed them in any dispute with the citizens.

There were two chief causes of friction. One was that the king had made the royal justices sitting at St. Martin's into a court of appeal from the Husting Court, if an error of judgment there was alleged. The Londoners could not deny the royal command, but they were very particular as to how appeal should be made. Several cases of appeal are recorded in the fourteenth century, but the city's reply was always the same: "The City of London does not allow a record in writing of any plaint in the Hustings Court to be sent to the justices at St. Martin-le-Grand; but after forty days for taking advice the mayor and aldermen will be prepared to report the case by word of mouth of the recorder as is the custom."

Where the citizens thought that a case would infringe the liberties of the city, the justices were met with flat opposition. Thus in 1325 a royal commission was sent to St. Martin to try a case of assault committed by some Londoners in Fleet Street. The mayor displayed the city charters to show that such a case should be tried by the city's own courts and refused to produce the defendants. A noted Londoner who benefited by the work of the court was John of Northampton. When John of Gaunt tried to secure his return to London from Tintagel, after his condemnation in 1384, Nicholas Brembre said that the city charters forbade it. After Brembre's execution in 1388, Gaunt tried again to restore his protegé, and in 1391 a court was held by the king's justices at St. Martin's when John of Northampton was declared innocent.

The second cause of friction in relation to St. Martin's was more inflaming because it was a source of almost daily irritation. The college of St. Martin claimed that by royal charters it was a specially powerful and inviolable sanctuary for fugitives from justice. Indeed it is said that when the king's justices came to St. Martin's and held their sessions in the Great South Gate on Newgate Street, the prisoners to be tried had to be marshaled on the opposite side of the road, for if they succeeded in crossing the channel in the middle of the road they could claim sanctuary in St. Martin's. This claim to sanctuary in the very heart of a great city was most exasperating to a government responsible for order in the city, for St. Martin's harbored a cluster of criminals who sallied forth at night to rob and then bolted back to St. Martin's when they were pursued. But as the privilege was ancient and backed by royal authority, the citizens had to put up with it.

In 1402 a petition to the king in Parliament complained that apprentices and servants carried off their masters' goods to St. Martin's and lived there on the money from the sale, that forgers worked in impunity there, that the residents bought goods in the city for which no payment could be had, and that robbers and murderers used it as a sure base for crime. The king ordered reasonable remedy to be given in his council, but nothing seems to have been done. Not only did robbers use St. Martin's as a base for crime, but counterfeiters used it as a place of manufacture. Faked goldsmith's work was made there in large quantities and then sold outside as genuine gold cups, rings, brooches, and chains. In the early fifteenth century the Londoners lost patience and raided the sanctuary on several occasions to remove criminals, but the dean and chapter always insisted on their rights, if necessary by appeal to the king. Indeed, in 1451 two men suspected of treason took refuge there and it was held that the privileges of St. Martin's held good even against the king himself.

But the dean and canons had carried matters too far, and six years later the king's council made some reforming ordinances for St. Martin's. Persons taking refuge there were to be registered; they must not keep their weapons; control must be exercised over criminals; stolen goods were to be restored to their owners; makers of counterfeit plate and jewels were not to be permitted in the sanctuary; men plying trades there must observe the rules of the city; and vice was not to be allowed. As so often with laws of that time, these rules were only imperfectly observed and the fundamental sanctuary rights still remained. Men often fled to sanctuary there—and sometimes missed it. In the reign of Richard III, Sir Roger Clifford, who had rebelled against him, was being drawn through the city, bound on a hurdle, to be beheaded on Tower Hill. His friar confessor was sorry for him and had unloosed his bonds so that when he was opposite St. Martin's he sprang up and made a dash for it. Clifford was within a few feet of success when the sheriff's men overpowered him and dragged him back to the hurdle, to complete the fatal journey.

For its part the chapter of St. Martin's had to accept city customs where they were clearly established, even against its own clergy. Thus in November, 1424, between eleven and twelve o'clock at night the constable and beadle of the parish of St. Stephen, Coleman Street, found Johanna, wife of the tailor Pascow Meneux, in bed with Richard Henney, a chaplain of St. Martin's. According to city custom he was made to stand in the pillory on Cornhill for an hour, even though he was a cleric, before he was handed over to the ecclesiastical authorities for discipline.

The intertwining of the jurisdiction of city and church is well illustrated by the life of St. Paul's. On the one hand the cathedral was a sanctuary and a consecrated building under the control of the cathedral dignitaries and chapter. On the other hand, as we have seen, serjeants-at-law used it as their accustomed office for meeting clients, tradesmen used it as a shop, one of the pillars was marked with a standard measure of length for the use of citizens, and the transepts served as a thoroughfare which Londoners claimed as a right of way by ancient custom.

In ecclesiastical law of the time the churchyard, as consecrated ground, was under the control of the church's authorities. But in Norman days the citizens had had the east side of the churchyard as the meeting place of the folkmoot. Although that had fallen into disuse by Chaucer's day, they still claimed the right to meet in the churchyard for the mustering of the militia. The churchyard wall was built partly by the bishops of London and partly by Edward II and Edward III; by the end of Chaucer's life it was becoming hidden by houses, both inside and outside, built by citizens of London, not by the dean and chapter. In 1282, Henry Waleys, the mayor, had made an agreement with the cathedral authorities that in return for the citizens' being allowed to build houses and shops next to the churchyard wall, they should contribute ten marks a year rent toward the building of a chapel of the Virgin Mary over the charnel house on the north side of the churchyard, where the bones of thousands of Londoners were stacked. The city was, moreover, to pay five marks a year rent toward the salary of the chaplain who celebrated masses there and could nominate a priest to the benefice. On the east side of the churchyard John Colet was, in 1512, to rebuild and endow St. Paul's School, but instead of putting the control in the hands of the chapter he gave the oversight and care of the endowments to the company of Mercers because his father was a former mercer and mayor.

Inside the church there were further reminders of the interconnection of church and city. Sir John Poultney, draper and four times mayor of London, ancestor of the earls of Bath, who died in 1349, had a chantry in St. Paul's; in his will he provided that the priest of the chantry should be nominated by the mayor of the year. In the next century Henry VI granted a patent for the incorporation of a guild in the crypt of St. Paul's, dedicated to the name of Jesus and under the direction of a rector and two wardens. From then until the Reformation, when the guild was suppressed, the rector was always the dean of the cathedral and the wardens were two city aldermen.

Not only did the citizens of London have much to do with the cathedral of which they were so proud, the canons had much to do with the life of London. The government of the cathedral by the fourteenth century was legally in the hands of the dignitaries—the dean, chancellor, precentor, treasurer, and for some purposes the archdeacons—and the thirty canons. In 1366, Pope Urban V made a determined enquiry into pluralism in the English Church, and as the returns for the province of Canterbury survive, it is possible to get an insight into what the members of the chapter were doing if they made a return, which twenty-four of them did. All but three of the twenty-four lived in London, but only eight or nine were resident canons attending daily to the services of the cathedral. Of these residentiaries, three were royal clerks and one was an ecclesiastical lawyer. Of the nonresidentiaries, no less than twelve were civil servants; three were officials of the Black Prince; one was in the household of Queen Philippa; one was to be later a clerk of John of Gaunt. All together twenty-one of the thirty-six members of the chapter were connected with the government, and it is hardly likely that those who did not even make a return were assiduous in the service of the cathedral church.

In spite of the absenteeism, or at any rate the rare attendances of the majority of the chapter, there were still plenty of clerics attached to St. Paul's needing to be governed. They were not easy to govern. There was, for example, in the late fourteenth century a prolonged battle between the bishop and the residentiary canons, or stagiaries. It had become customary to burden the stagiary in his first year of office with enormous entertainment expenses. Besides frequent invitations to fellow stagiaries and junior ministers, he was expected to keep open house each day at breakfast time and to give a great feast twice in that year. To this he had to invite the bishop and all the canons, the mayor and aldermen, justices and important royal officials, to maintain the friendship between the city and the Church and to seek the favor of the royal court.

The stagiaries appropriated to themselves a large part of the revenues of the cathedral to meet these expenses, and this in turn annoyed the nonresidentiaries, many of whom (as we have seen) had influence with the king. In 1371 the king at their instigation, acting on behalf of the founders of St. Paul's, issued letters patent denouncing in rhetorical terms the greed of the stagiaries and chiding the bishop for allowing such abuses. In emotional language the royal message described how in the olden days the brewhouse had been a center of alms, whereas now it was broken up into workshops and brothels and its revenues were diverted to the stagiaries.

The bishop at this time was the gentle Simon Sudbury,

who as archbishop was to be beheaded in the Peasants Revolt. His successors as bishops of London, William Courtenay and Robert Braybrooke, were made of sterner stuff. Courtenay dealt firmly with Wycliffe and the Lollards, including the famous arraignment of Wycliffe at a court in St. Paul's in 1377, when the court broke up in confusion after the altercation between Courtenay and John of Gaunt.

Braybrooke hit with equal force at the condition of the cathedral. In 1385 he issued an ordinance to stop buying and selling inside the cathedral, the playing of ball games and the throwing of stones in the churchyard (as these practices were doing great damage to the windows and images), and the shooting of birds on the cathedral walls. In 1392 he succeeded after much effort in getting a papal bull which denounced the lavish entertainment obligations of the stagiaries in their first year as monstrous excesses, estimated their cost at 700 to 1,000 marks a year (equivalent to the revenue of some bishops), and declared these expenses abolished. In their place was to be a fixed entry fine of 300 marks as a contribution to the chapter funds. The response of the stagiaries seems to have been a silent but determined passive resistance; perhaps because of this their number had sunk to one by 1400. The aging bishop roused himself to action and before he died in 1404 he had appointed a new dean and at least three other residentiaries. But the problem remained of how to attract suitable recruits when there were so many temptations to extravagance and nonresidence, and how to provide adequately for both stagiaries and nonresident canons from the cathedral revenues. There was to be a further struggle about the entry fine and it took two further papal bulls to enforce it.

If there were few stagiaries, this does not mean that the cathedral services were neglected. Toward the end of the thirteenth century we first clearly discern the institution of twelve minor canons who, by Chaucer's time, were already men of consequence in the cathedral close and in the city outside. The two most senior were known by the impressive title of cardinal and from their ranks were chosen the officials who did most of the actual organization of the cathedral and its services: the subdean, sacrist, succentor, chamberlain, and almoner. The men of the fourteenth century were favorably disposed toward the founding of corporate bodies such as university colleges, inns of court, and bodies of priests. In 1353 the minor canons joined together to found a common hall with houses attached—somewhat like the Vicars' Close that still exists at Wells, but without its peace and calm. Bishop Braybrooke was much concerned, as we have seen, to reform the government of the cathedral, and in 1395–96 he arranged for the incorporation of the minor canons under the control of the dean and chapter.

The minor canons could be expected to control the vicars' choral and the choristers, but the numerous and unruly chantry priests were a different problem. There had been a spate of chantry founding, especially after the Black Death, of 1348–49, and by 1366 St. Paul's had no less than seventy-four. Bishop Braybrooke said that many of them were so poor that their chaplains had to become vicars of city and country churches to eke out their living, but most contemporaries seem not to have agreed with him. There was a widespread view that a chantry in St. Paul's was a lucrative job with only light duties. Langland made a famous complaint in his *Vision of Piers Plowman* that parish priests were deserting their congregations and going to St. Paul's to seek for chantries. Chaucer confirms this view in his statement about his ideal parson:

> *He sette nat his benefice to hyre,*
> *And leet his sheep encombred in the myre,*
> *And ran to London, unto seynt Poules,*
> *To seken him a chaunterie for soules,*
> *Or with a bretherhed to been withholde;*
> *But dwelte at hoom, and kepte wel his folde.*

The returns of pluralists in 1366 show that six of the chantry chaplains held livings outside the diocese, but all of them lived in London. Of thirty-one chaplains for whom we have information, all but three held other livings as well and sixteen of them held city churches. Everybody, except the chaplains themselves, agreed that they were a problem for the Church and for London. It was said that some of them were unruly, that many of them spent too much time in London taverns, and that some were a danger to the morals of respectable London women. Such charges may have been exaggerated, but they may have encouraged a group of chaplains to build for themselves, in the early fourteenth century, a communal house north of the cathedral which came to be known as St. Peter's College. In 1391, Bishop Braybrooke reduced the number of chaplains and incorporated them in the college, which was to be under the control of the dean and chapter.

Whether the college achieved all that Braybrooke hoped of it is hard to tell. The fifteenth century seems to have been a time of greater order in the affairs of the chantry priests than the fourteenth century had been. But to achieve complete regularity was extraordinarily difficult, if not impossible, in the circumstances. Not only were the dean and chapter, who were ultimately responsible for good order and government in the precinct, mostly absentees, as we have seen, but the precinct was bound up with the teeming life of London. Apart from the minor canons, vicars, choirboys, and chantry priests, the precinct was thronged daily with a host of other officials and servants: vergers, surveyors, scribes, bookbinders, brewers, bakers, and bedesmen, not to speak of the milling crowds of Londoners. Londoners might grumble at the unruliness of St. Paul's churchyard, exempt from city authority, at the wealth of the canons, at the idleness and comforts of the numerous chantry priests; but they themselves contributed greatly to the encroachments of the world on the cathedral both inside and out, and they welcomed the patronage of its clergy. They were proud of their cathedral, which they regarded as very much their own, and they regarded it as second to none.

][ ][ ][

The Society of London

It is clear that by Chaucer's day the guild system was of
great importance for the whole fabric of London society.
This does not mean that all, or even most, of the inhabitants were full members of guilds and enjoyed through
them the rights of citizenship. It is very hard to say what
was the exact proportion. Let us take the figures from
Henry VIII's reign as a start, because these are much
fuller than anything available for the fourteenth century,
even though inadequate.

In 1537 the total number of freeman householders was
about three thousand. If we allow an average of five members to a household, we get a figure for the citizen class
of about fifteen thousand and the total population of London at that time has been estimated at about sixty thousand. The proportion of freemen in the fourteenth century
is unlikely to have been greater; indeed, to judge from
the comparative number of apprentices it was probably
less. It therefore seems that, at a generous estimate, for
every freeman there were in Chaucer's London at least

three adult men unenfranchised. The latter were called "foreigns" and were of at least four different kinds.

The growing power and prosperity of the London guilds caused increasingly open resentment against alien merchants. In 1327 young Edward III, anxious to placate the Londoners, granted them a charter that forced aliens to sell their goods within forty days and to board with English hosts, who could watch their movements. In 1335, when he was firmly on his throne and needed the aliens, he conferred full freedom of trade on all merchants. This act was renewed in 1351, but it was increasingly unpopular in London and when discontent spilled over in the Good Parliament of 1376 the Londoners complained that aliens were impoverishing the city and that they spied out the secrets of the realm.

The reign of Richard II was a confused period in which there were rapid reversals of policy, with the victualing guilds trying to enforce restrictions on aliens whenever they had the power to do so. They wanted merchant aliens coming to England to be treated as English merchants were treated abroad. They were anxious that foreign merchants should not be allowed to sell retail and that they should not be permitted to carry gold or silver out of the realm.

There were increasingly frequent attacks on aliens. There was a murderous attack against Lombards in Old Jewry at midsummer, 1359, and during the Peasants Revolt many Flemings were beheaded in the streets of London. The Hanseatic merchants seem to have fared better because they had their strongly fortified enclosure and took great care how and when they ventured into the streets of London. But they, too, were strangers in a foreign land, isolated and excluded from London society. The Flemings mingled more with the Londoners, with complex results. On the one hand, we hear of social intercourse between them and Londoners; on the other hand, in a royal proclamation of 1369 the king could say that evil and insult were daily inflicted on the Flemings.

If they were wealthy and influential, aliens had some chance of royal protection and the prospect of going home again as soon as they could. They were thus in a far better position than that of the second category of "foreigns," poor aliens without protection and without the means to go home, and native craftsmen, often from outside London. They were too poor to become guild members and thus acquire the rights of setting up shop, employing labor, and taking apprentices. Such men sometimes tried to carry on trade illegally, but in such a tightly knit community it was very difficult to do this without being detected—unless one operated in the slums of Southwark or Westminster, or the east end outside the city where control was slacker. Most of these poor craftsmen seem, however, to have earned their living by working for established freemen. Their lives were precarious; for unlike apprentices, their conditions of service were not protected by guild regulations. The master craftsmen issued scales of wages for them; for example, the master weavers in 1407 enacted that workmen were to receive 5d a day, without food or drink.

In their way of life they merged into the third category

of "foreigns," the laboring classes, who supplied the domestic servants, porters, and boatmen needed by the merchants and craftsmen to fetch and carry for them. The most fortunate members of this class were those who could form a stable relationship with established craftsmen, obeying all their orders and wishes and receiving protection and maintenance for faithful service. The outlook and way of life of the craftsmen were therefore decisive in the lives of these laborers.

The luckiest, in terms of standards of living, were those who lived in the houses of their employers, as many of the craftsmen and servants did. They would not have understood the twentieth-century repugnance to this on the grounds of "lack of freedom to live their own lives." A full stomach, a warm fire, and a comfortable bed were far more desirable than freedom to be cold and hungry. A poor craftsman or a laborer was lucky if, like Langland, he had a small cottage of his own, though even this was often only a two-room dwelling with an earthen floor that became messy in winter from trampling of wet feet, with no chimney to take away the smoke, no glass to keep out the wind, and built of thin wood planking that did not keep out the winter cold and was liable to quick decay. Many laborers are described as living on someone's "rents," which means that they had one or two rooms in what would now be described as a tenement house. Since the ground floor was often useful to the owner as a shop or a workroom, the living accommodation would often be either on an upper floor or in a cellar. If it was on an upper floor, it was often reached, in this type of house, by an outside staircase or a ladder, which led to accidents to old folks, children, and drunkards and hence to mention in the coroners' rolls. If the accommodation was in a cellar, the approach was by a stairway which, like the ladder, projected into the street and formed, like the ladder, a further hazard on dark nights.

Where possessions are described, they are, not surprisingly, scanty: tables and beds of planks, a few pots and pans of copper and brass, a few blankets and sheets, a few shirts and frieze gowns. Occasionally a thrifty workman might invest in a silver cup or some silver spoons to be sold if disaster came.

Even less influential in shaping London society were the considerable numbers of people below these more fortunate and steady laboring men and women. The coroners' and jail delivery rolls, the letter books and mayor's court records, all give glimpses of a mass of destitution, knavery, hard fortune, and poverty, housed in tumbledown buildings in slums and alleys. Some of these folk earned a precarious living as casual laborers; some were tricksters and thieves who haunted taverns, especially in Southwark. Some were blind, lame, or diseased, dependent on the charity of pious benefactors. Some were soldiers, like Bardolf, waiting for the next campaign.

The criminal elements were the cause of much pickpocketing and made the streets dangerous on moonless nights; all men of any standing agreed that they must be kept sternly under control. The penalty for theft of goods valued at more than one shilling could be death. If a thief was a first offender and not a member of what were regarded as the criminal classes, the goods were often valued at less than 12d in order to give him another chance. Typical cases recorded in the letter books are those of Alan and Thomas, both from York, who had no chattels and were hanged for the theft of rayed cloth in 1343 and Simon Wylde, hanged for the theft of various goods in 1378, who had a coverlet and sheet valued at 6d.

Often the thefts involved considerable penetration of houses or other property. In 1337, Desiderata de Toryntone got into the household of Lady Alice de Lisle and stole some silver saltcellars and dishes while Lady Alice was at the Bishop of Salisbury's house in Fleet Street. In 1341 Stephen Salle crept at twilight on board the ship of a Dordrecht captain while it was tied up at the Wool Wharf and stole articles valued at 6s/8d. Both Desiderata and Stephen were condemned to be hanged; neither had any chattels. Some indication of the numbers of the very poor is given by the bequest of Robert de Lincoln in 1318 of a penny each to two thousand poor people, or by the vastness of the crowd that thronged the gate of Blackfriars in 1322 for the distribution of alms, when fifty people were trampled to death.

Many persons resorted to imposture and swindling; their punishment was usually the pillory. Fourteenth-century London did not believe in spending the citizens' money on expensive imprisonment; if the offender was not to be eliminated from society by hanging, it was better to save expense by putting him in the pillory where he would suffer ridicule, and perhaps missiles, and be a warning example to others. So the pillory was used for all kinds of impostures: for pretending to be one of the sheriffs' serjeants, the summoner of the Archbishop of Canterbury, the king's purveyor, a holy hermit, an officer of the Marshalsea. It was also the punishment for swindling: begging under false pretences, deceiving the public with counters for gold, practicing soothsaying and magic, or counterfeiting the bulls and seals of the pope.

Sometimes the impostures and swindlings were elaborate. In 1380 two imposters who pretended to be mute went around London with a piece of leather shaped like a tongue, an iron hook and pincers, and two ell measures. By signs they gave observers to believe that (as shown by their ell measures) they were traders who had been robbed, that their tongues had been drawn out by the hook and cut off with the pincers. They made roaring noises and opened their mouths to show that they had no tongues. When found out, they were stood in the pillory for three successive days with the instruments round their necks and were then remanded to Newgate until further notice. Then there was the pretended physician in 1382, Roger Clerk, who persuaded Roger atte Hacche of Ironmonger Lane to let him heal his wife Johanna of fever by hanging a parchment round her neck. Clerk had said that there was a charm written on the rolled up parchment, but when unrolled in court it was found to be blank and he was discovered, on cross-examination, to be illiterate. He was condemned to ride around the city on a horse without a saddle, the parchment hung about his neck and urinals (symbol of the physician then) hung before and behind him, with trumpeters and pipers accompanying him to draw attention to his offense.

In all their attempts at suppressing crime the city authorities could count on the king's support. In 1340 a porter wounded one of the city sergeants in a riot and was forthwith condemned to death by the mayor at the Guildhall. Edward III wrote to the mayor to commend him for his prompt action.

By contrast with the members of these depressed classes of Londoners, a boy who was fortunate enough to be apprenticed to a craft was on his way to reaching a secure position in London society. It is true that membership of a craft involved obligations at every stage. When a boy was admitted to apprenticeship, his master had to pay a fee which varied a good deal in amount from the 1s of the Carpenters to the 20s of the Skinners. But great or small, it meant that for a considerable number of years (often seven but sometimes as many as twelve) the young man was subject to close control by his master, dwelling in his house and working under his eye. The master craftsman had to provide living conditions deemed suitable for an apprentice and had to train him in the craft, receiving in turn a premium from the boy's family. If the master was negligent or harsh, it was possible for the boy or his parents to complain not only to the wardens of the craft, but to the city government and to the law courts. There are cases in the early Chancery proceedings of fathers complaining that their sons had not been educated as they should have been or that they had been forced to perform menial duties.

In a case in Chancery about 1445 we find William Grene complaining that Sir William Capell, to whom his son had been apprenticed, had misused the lad in this way. Sir William had promised in the apprenticeship agreement, said Grene, that Thomas should never be used "as a keeper of his horses, bearer of his tankards, nor to do any such vile and bestial service which would be any abasement to the said apprentice, considering that he was a gentleman and allied to many worshipful persons." Yet this is what Sir William is said to have done "to the great disgrace of the said apprentice, which was presumably the cause of his great illness."

Thomas had a determined father, but this was not always the case. There was clearly a temptation for some masters to make use of their apprentices as cheap labor and there are instances in the fourteenth century of some apprentices being kept in their apprenticeship for fourteen years. Yet the system did not degenerate into uncontrolled child labor. City regulations were concerned to prevent that by insisting on adequate living conditions and training, restricting the number of apprentices that a master could take, and requiring him to present them for the freedom of the city at the end of their term. Some crafts were stricter than others in their supervision of labor. At times the Skinners had a high proportion of apprentices who either did not complete their training or were never sufficiently prosperous to set up as masters; between 1391 and 1464 nearly half the enrolled apprentices of the Mercers seem to have failed to become freemen of the company.

Naturally the government of a craft, in that hierarchical society, took a very strict view of insubordination, especially if accompanied by violence. Punishment for this offense could be expulsion, with the alternative of whipping as a lesser retribution. In 1430, for example, the wardens of the Goldsmiths Company were asked to hear a case brought by a master goldsmith, John Hille, who had intended to chastise his apprentice John Richard for some offense, whereupon the young man had snatched up a window pole and threatened to kill him. Hille left the house at once for help and Richard was promptly arrested. No one else would take him as an apprentice and he was condemned to leave the craft and the city.

Compared with this bleak fate, the treatment given to William Bowden was probably regarded as merciful. In 1456 he was brought before the wardens of the Goldsmiths Company accused of having beaten his mistress, causing blood to flow. He was condemned to be led into the kitchen of the hall and there stripped naked and, by the hand of his master, to be beaten until he was bloody. "Nakyd as he was betyn," the apprentice, still kneeling, had to ask pardon of his master and mistress.

But it was not often that relations between masters and apprentices came to such extremes. Unlike the relationships between employer and employee in our society, often quite impersonal, the connections between master and apprentice were very close. They commonly slept in the same bedroom, they certainly worked side by side, and often the master developed something of a paternal affection for his apprentice. Several of the wills proved in the Hustings Court record bequests from masters to apprentices and display a spirit of goodwill. For example, in 1385, Sir William Walworth left in his will £40 each to his two apprentices, £5 each to his former apprentice John Whithered and Matilda his wife, besides £100 to the Carthusians for a chantry for the soul of his former master John Lovekyn. At the end of the term most masters seem to have been glad to present their apprentices for the freedom of the city and some masters paid the necessary fee for the apprentice.

What happened to the young man after that depended on a combination of wealth, social standing, skill, good relations with his master, and luck—and luck included staying alive during the plagues which were recurrent and devastating. There were three bad outbreaks in the 1360's, and during the third and fourth decades of the fifteenth century there were six serious attacks.

If the young man survived this hazard, he might advance his fortunes most rapidly if he could make a profitable marriage. An ambitious young man made business-like inquiries, took his time, and even paid a marriage broker if necessary. Even if he came of a careful family, he had to have luck on his side. In 1385, for example, we find Walter Doget, vintner, trying to give his son a start by a careful marriage. Lands and tenements to the value of the considerable sum of £300 were to be bought for the son, John Doget, and Idonea, his wife, partly by a contribution of £100 from Walter Doget, partly by £100 from Idonea's dead father, and partly by £100 from her stepfather John Philpot. But in 1394, Henry Vanner, another vintner and trustee of the settlement, came into court and asked for the bond to be canceled since both Walter Doget and Idonea had died.

Of course, most young husbands could expect to be more fortunate. If a man could marry a wealthy widow and use her children's patrimony for trading purposes, he might make his fortune. But there was great competition for heiresses and widows and a man might easily be unsuccessful in the race. If he had no capital, initiative, or luck, he might have to continue in service to the end of his days. Even if he became an independent master, he might not be admitted to the inner circle of the craft which, as described in the previous chapter, was becoming its real government.

Perhaps it was because the fraternities of the guilds were becoming so important in the latter half of the fourteenth century that we hear less of the Fraternity of the Pui. This was a social guild that flourished in the late thirteenth and early fourteenth centuries, and had included mayors and other persons of the ruling class among its members. Its main function was ostensibly to hold a great feast each summer on the Sunday following Trinity Sunday. The members of the feast were to elect a new "Prince" who then presided over a festival of songs. Each member submitted a song or paid 12d, and the song deemed the best was "crowned." The Pui supported a chaplain to sing for the souls of its members and a clerk to keep their records; poor members were to be helped from the common funds. Undoubtedly it was deemed an honor to be a member, but one suspects that membership was exclusive.

By the latter half of the century the Londoner's gregarious urges were better served. If a man could not gain admittance to the ruling fraternity of the guild he might find companionship and fulfillment in the lesser fraternity of the craft. In the 1390's the lesser craftsmen, or yeomanry, of the Skinners combined to form the Fraternity of Our Lady's Assumption, and they seem to have outnumbered their more exclusive brethren who belonged to the Fraternity of Corpus Christi. Of 1,047 recorded freemen of the Mercers Company between 1391 and 1464, only 456 were admitted to the livery.

So long as such a yeoman fraternity would accept subordination to the ruling group that was soon to become the livery company, it was left to manage its own affairs. This gave scope for leading members to express and develop their personalities. They could become officials of the fraternity—as one of its wardens or perhaps its clerk—and they joined together in dinners, commemorative masses and funerals, the relief of the sick and the poor. A common provision was to provide sick pay when a member was ill, usually after he had made a minimum number of contributions. The rules of the Brotherhood of Carpenters, made in 1333, are typical of many later ones. If any brother or sister should fall sick, then the brotherhood was to pay 14d each week after the member had lain sick for a fortnight; if the common fund had not enough to pay for the sick, then more was to be collected from the healthy. If a brother was unemployed, he was to be employed by a guildsman in preference to anyone else.

By Chaucer's time another kind of guild, the parish guild, was opening up opportunities of comradeship to lesser craftsmen. Only eight or nine are known to have existed in London before 1350, whereas another thirty-eight were founded before the end of the century and twenty-seven more were established in the fifteenth and early sixteenth centuries. Like the craft guilds, the parish guilds enabled men to feel that they had a respected place in the society of their city. Such guilds cannot have included the down-and-out elements, for all demanded an entrance fee and regularity of behavior, and usually they asked for some pride in appearance in the form of a simple uniform or livery for formal occasions. Their rules often breathed the spirit of hard work and sobriety appropriate to people who were just reaching a secure and respectable status in society. For example, the guild of St. Anne in the parish of St. Lawrence Jewry threatened to expel any member who wasted his time drinking in taverns, lying in bed too long, or frequenting wrestling matches when he should have been earning a living for himself and his family.

By contemporary standards a parish guild could do much for a man. It made him feel that he belonged to a community of both living and dead, which would continue to care for his soul when he, too, had died. One of the most common obligations of membership was to attend mass on the day of the patronal festival and on the burial of one of the fraternity. Each member made an offering on such an occasion and paid quarterly subscriptions. The funds created from this and other sources enabled the fraternity to pay for a free funeral and requiem mass for any brother or sister who had died too poor to provide for himself or herself.

By the end of the century, when the parish guilds had become so numerous, it was possible to choose a guild, either in one's own parish or a neighboring one, to suit one's purse and status. Sometimes guilds of differing social status existed in the same church. Thus in the church of St. Sepulchre, beyond Newgate, there existed by the early fifteenth century a guild for the more affluent. It maintained a chaplain to celebrate mass continually, it supported a perpetually burning light before the image of St. Stephen, and any member who fell into poverty that was not his own fault received 14d a week. All the brethren assembled for mass on St. Stephen's Day and offered at least a farthing; on the following Sunday they met for a feast and wore "cowls of a suit." When a brother died, the guild was wealthy enough to provide tapers for his requiem mass and three rentals of masses to be sung for his soul. The guild of the Conception of the Blessed Virgin Mary at the same church could not afford a permanent chantry, but hired a priest for the annual festival and for funerals. It could afford to pay only 6d a week to members in distress.

Like the trade guilds, these parish guilds often developed a social security aspect. They would often pay sickness benefits to ailing members, and they urged guildsmen to employ unemployed brethren in preference to anyone else. St. Katherine's fraternity at St. Botolph's Aldersgate made loans to those needing a small amount. The guild of St. Fabian and St. Sebastian in the same church helped its young members to find work. The Fraternity of St. Mary's in All Hallows, London Wall, was willing to give legal or charitable help to any member whose son or daughter had been unfairly treated by any master to whom he or she had been apprenticed—clearly catering to members who could put their children into guild apprenticeship. A common provision was for the guild to adjudicate in matters of dispute between its members, thus saving them the expense of a lawsuit. It is true that an entrance fee of 5s was a deterrent for some, and after that the quarterly payments had to be kept up. But to judge by the proliferation of parish and trade guilds in the London of Chaucer's day, a great number of citizens not only wanted this kind of association, but found it possible to belong to one.

It is a commonplace that the effect of the Church on society was great in Chaucer's time, but its relationship was especially intimate in London. Intimate, but not always harmonious. There was a conservative strain in the city's life which caused the city government to claim control, against the wishes of the Church authorities, over sexual offenses, whether committed by laymen or clerics. Action was taken in the Mayor's Court against adulterers, bawds, courtesans, and whoremongers. A male offender was at the first offense to have his hair and beard shaved off except for a fringe two inches wide round his head; for the second offense he was to be put in the pillory and thereafter ten days in prison; and for the third offense he was to be expelled from the city. A priest who was caught with a woman was to be brought to the Tun prison in Cornhill, attended by minstrels, and after the third offense to be driven out of the city.

The city was also very attached to its ancient rights, which it was prepared to enforce against the Church, if need be. When in 1378 the rector of the church of St. Michael le Querne blocked up the doorway of the church with a stone wall, to stop people using it as a thoroughfare, the Common Serjeant presented the rector and the four men who had helped him to the mayor and aldermen in the Chamber of the Guildhall. The mayor and aldermen decreed, under penalty of £20 for each person, that the wall should be pulled down and that the old door should stand open for the common passage of the people through the church.

A very different effect of the Church's teachings on the citizens was the provision of chantries and the rebuilding of the parish churches. The numerous fraternities which sprang up in the late fourteenth century all had a chantry element, i.e., masses for the faithful departed. In addition to these, the age of Chaucer saw a remarkable growth in the number of chantries founded for the souls of individuals and their families. In the fourteenth century, on an average, twenty-eight permanent chantries were founded in London every ten years. We have already noted the great number of chantries at St. Paul's; by the end of the century most of the parish churches had more than one chantry. St. Michael's, Crooked Lane, had so many that Sir William Walworth combined them in 1380 into a college with a master and nine priests.

The chantries and fraternities between them caused an increased use of the altars of parish churches and created a desire to extend the edifices, where the site permitted, by adding aisles to accommodate more altars. The growing wealth of London made this possible, and between 1300 and 1450 at least fifty parish churches were rebuilt, enlarged, or extensively repaired. In this period Londoners were enriching their churches with glass, books, vestments, and furnishings such as silver plate, pyxes, crucifixes, candlesticks, bells, lecterns, roodbeams, parclose screens, and even pulpits. They were also increasing endowments, so that whereas London churches had in the twelfth century been on the whole rather poor, by the early sixteenth century they were on the whole rich.

By 1450 most of the parish churches had two or three priests besides the rector; several had seven or more, and a few had twelve. Some of this activity was financed by the fraternities. At St. Magnus by the Bridge, for example, the Fraternity of Salve Regina, founded about 1354 to support an anthem of Our Lady every evening, with five tapers burning for the five joys of the Virgin, took the lead in rebuilding this church "because it was too small to receive all the people and was old and ruinous." It became one of the wealthy churches of London. In other cases leading citizens contributed heavily. Because the old site of St. Stephen's was too small, two aldermen gave land for a new church on the other side of the Walbrook and in 1429 the twelve foundation stones were laid by the mayor, six aldermen, the churchwardens, and others. Twenty years earlier Richard Whittington had started to rebuild his parish church of St. Michael Paternoster and his executors founded a college of five priests there. Among those who assisted in the rebuilding, endowment, and enriching of parish churches were the craft guilds. The way in which the Salters helped in the extension of All Hallows, Bread Street, or the Skinners in the rebuilding of St. John's, Walbrook, is impressive. The enrichments were varied. By the time of the Reformation, St. Margaret, New Fish Street, had, among many other relics, pieces of the burning bush and Moses' rod, part of the manger and crib of Our Lord, the stole, gloves, and comb of St. Dunstan, and a tooth of St. Bridget.

The connections between the social and economic life of the city and the Church are to be observed in another way. We have seen that a common obligation of the members of a fraternity was to attend mass together on the feast day of their patron saint, and there was a strong desire to have a common uniform or livery to wear on such occasions. Even the poorer parish fraternities tried to achieve this. It was therefore unlikely that the more exclusive craft fraternities forming in Chaucer's day would neglect such a fashionable habit. The regulations of the craft fraternities were in fact insistent on the necessity for all members to equip themselves with the latest livery. By the early fifteenth century the wealthier guilds were changing their livery every two or three years, the second best being kept for less solemn occasions. At this time the combination of colors was vivid; the Grocers had scarlet and green, scarlet and black, scarlet and deep blue, scarlet and violet. The dyes were usually expensive and so were the cloths of which the liveries were made; it was a good way of displaying the wealth and importance of one's guild.

Processions to church on the patronal day, with guildsmen in their resplendent newest livery, therefore came to be a common feature of the social life of the guilds and of London in the late fourteenth century. Indeed, it commended itself so much that some guilds had not one but two or three processions. The first took place by torchlight on the eve of the saint's day, and the guildsmen heard a requiem mass for the repose of the souls of the deceased men and women of the fraternity. Then on the festival day itself there was another procession to the parish church for a high mass. This was followed by a procession in state to some large room for a dinner. In Chaucer's time most guilds still had to hire a room in an inn for this purpose, but one of the many attractions of owning a hall was that it gave greater prestige to the event.

The possession of a hall was all the more useful in that it was coming to be the custom for the dinner to be followed by the election of the master and wardens of the guild for the coming year. The retiring master and wardens would enter with garlands on their heads, preceded by the guild's beadle and by minstrels. These garlands or chaplets seem to have been relatively simple at this time, but by the sixteenth century they had commonly become expensive creations of velvet and ermine, elaborately embroidered with leaves, flowers, and coats of arms in gold, silver, and other colored threads. The oldest surviving chaplet, dated 1561, is said to have belonged to the Carpenters Company. After a mock display of indecision, the garlands were placed on the heads of those who had in fact already been chosen as master and wardens for the coming year. The oath of office was administered and the former master and wardens drank to the health of their successors. Even the masters who were not members of the ruling fraternity, as well as the journeymen of the craft, were usually allowed to watch this proceeding, which was both a colorful social event and a dignified ceremony emphasizing the guild's prestige.

To have a procession to church on the guild's patronal day, followed by an election and feast, was not the limit of what could be done to emphasize the guild's importance. It could stress its connection with the city government. There were different ways in which this could be attempted. One especially effective stroke was to gain for one's craft the right to organize the city's public celebration of some important feast day. We have seen how the dominant set of masters in the skinners' guild was organizing itself into the Fraternity of Corpus Christi in the fourteenth century. Its charter of 1393 confirmed the right, which it had evidently exercised already for many years, of organizing the Corpus Christi procession in the city. Stow tells us how "This fraternitie had also once every yere on Corpus Christi day after noone a Procession, passed through the principall streetes of the Citie, wherein was borne more than one hundred Torches of Waxe (costly garnished) burning light, and above two hundred Clearkes and Priests in Surplesses and Coapes, singing. After the which were the shiriffes servants, the Clarkes of the Counters, Chaplains for the Shiriffes, the Maiors Sargeants, the counsell of the Citie, the Maior and Aldermen in scarlet, and then the Skinners in their best Liveryes." What better method could have been devised to stress to the city the importance of the Skinners? But most guilds did not have this combination of wealth and luck; for most the best policy was to insert themselves into the mayoral processions on major saints' days.

By the late fourteenth century there were a good many of these processions, especially to the church of St. Thomas Acon. On the north side of Cheap, a little to the east of St. Mary-le-Bow, St. Thomas Becket had been born, and after the martyrdom his sister Agnes and her husband had given the site for the foundation of a hospital of the Military Order of St. Thomas of Acon. Gifts poured in to obtain the prayers of a famous saint who might be expected to have a special regard for his native city and the hospital became wealthy. The city government was glad to emphasize its connection with the famous martyr, its patron saint, and in 1327 the custody of the hospital was transferred to the mayor and commonalty. In 1383 they caused the church to be rebuilt on a bigger scale, with side aisles and several chapels, in the fashionable Perpendicular Gothic style. In winter there was a series of civic processions to St. Thomas Acon for mass and thence to St. Paul's for vespers and compline—

on All Hallows Day (November 1), Christmas Day, St. Stephen's, St. John's, and Holy Innocents' Days (December 26, 27, and 28), Circumcision (January 1), Epiphany (January 6), and Purification (February 2). At Easter the mayor, aldermen, and sheriffs went to St. Mary Bethlehem Hospital outside Bishopsgate. On Whitmonday they visited St. Peter's Cornhill and, led by all the rectors of the city churches, they then marched in procession to the graveyard of St. Paul's to pray at the tomb of the parents of St. Thomas Becket. There they were received by the clergy of the cathedral and the Archdeacon of London gave two nobles (gold coins) to the serjeants-at-mace of the city. On the Whittuesday and Whitwednesday there were mayoral processions from other city churches to St. Paul's, where the Archdeacon of Middlesex had to pay the serjeants-at-mace 10s on the Tuesday, and the Archdeacon of Essex had to present 6s/8d to them on the Wednesday.

Londoners valued these processions greatly and insisted on the correct uniform or livery. In 1382 it was ordained that the mayor and aldermen should all wear cloaks of green, lined with green taffeta, for the Whitmonday procession; when the alderman of Walbrook ward appeared wearing a cloak without a lining, he was condemned to entertain the mayor and all the aldermen to dinner the following Tuesday. Londoners also set store by precedence in these processions. For years there was a dispute between the parishioners of St. Peter's Cornhill, St. Magnus the Martyr, and St. Nicholas Cole Abbey regarding which of their respective rectors should have precedence in the Whitmonday procession. It is no wonder that the leading guilds not only wanted a place in the procession but desired as favorable a position as possible.

The most important civic event of the year was the election of the mayor, and it was a matter of special consequence to the guilds to have their due place in the procession. Due place meant appropriate precedence. The election occurred each year at the Guildhall on the Feast of St. Simon and St. Jude (October 28). On the morrow of the feast the new and the former mayor, together with the sheriffs and aldermen in their liveries and the leading men of the crafts in their liveries, assembled on horseback at the Guildhall at nine in the morning. They rode along Cheapside, through Newgate, down to Fleet Street, along the Strand to Westminster, where they dismounted. Then they went into the Exchequer, where they were met by the Chancellor, Treasurer, and Keeper of the Privy Seal, with the Barons of the Exchequer. The Recorder then announced the name of the new mayor, who repeated his oath of office, promised to keep the peace of the city, to see that the price of food was controlled, and to account at the Exchequer for his profits as Escheator. Having appointed attorneys at the Exchequer, Common Pleas, and King's Bench, he returned to London. In front of him rode the leading men of the guilds in their liveries, the members of his own guild immediately preceding him. The mayor was surrounded by the serjeants-at-arms, mace bearers, sword bearer, and sheriffs, and was followed by the recorder and aldermen.

These ceremonies on the occasion of the mayor's election met such a psychological need of Londoners that they were to have a great development. In the middle of the fifteenth century the mayor began to travel to Westminster by water in a splendid state barge. So important had the procession become to the guilds that a great feud developed between the Merchant Taylors and the Skinners about which of their barges had precedence. From the sixteenth century the procession through the city was adorned with pageantry that developed into the Lord Mayor's Show as we know it today.

In the age of Chaucer civic pageantry, though not as yet associated with the mayoral procession, was already developing. It provided free entertainment to the Londoners and flattered their civic pride—and it could be made to advertise the wealth and competence of the guilds. When Richard II was crowned in 1377, the goldsmiths organized a pageant. They erected in Cheapside an elaborate castle with four towers, on each of which stood a beautiful maiden. When the king rode through Cheapside on his way from the Tower to Westminster, these virgins blew leaves of gold on him and threw artificial gold coins before him and his horses. Wine in abundance ran from two sides of the castle; between the towers was placed a gold angel, so contrived that when the king came, it bowed down and offered him a crown. Altogether the goldsmiths spent nearly £13 on this coronation pageant, more than double the minimum annual wage of a curate or chaplain. These elements—the elaborate structure, the maidens, the flowing wine, the mechanism, and the gifts—were all to be features of later pageants.

The goldsmiths' device of 1377 was apparently used again when Anne of Bohemia came to England in 1382; but before long the citizens were marking an important event by having more than one "device" in the pageantry. In 1392 the city was anxious for the royal forgiveness after the king's seizure of the government into his own hand. The citizens thought it politic to placate him with pageantry and gifts. As he and the queen approached London Bridge from Southwark, they met him and presented a milk-white steed caparisoned in red and cloth-of-gold. As the royal party passed through the city, the conduits ran with wine, and between the cross in Cheapside and St. Paul's there was a stage on which many angels stood and sang. An angel came down a staircase and put crowns of gold, set with pearls and other precious stones, on the heads of the king and queen. There was another ornamental stage at the door of St. Paul's, with a chorus of angels and God Himself. At Temple Bar the royal party encountered a stage built to represent a "desert" on which stood St. John the Baptist and all kinds of strange beasts. Next day the citizens completed their reconciliation by going to Westminster and presenting the king with two basins of silver gilt, containing coins to the value of £10,000.

Under the Lancastrians the pageantry grew more splendid. Henry IV had great ridings at his coronation in 1399 and his marriage in 1403. But these were far outdone by the celebrations for Henry V after his return from Agincourt and those for Henry VI on his return from his coronation in Paris in 1432 as King of France. The rejoicings after Agincourt were so great that it took the king and his followers five hours to travel from Blackheath to Westminster. From the hour when he crossed London Bridge to the time when he left the city at Temple Bar, he and his small band slowly made their way through dense and cheering crowds. At every important stage of the route they encountered archways and castles decked with bunting and painted scenery, adorned with impersonations of saints and patriarchs, kings and nobles, angels and cherubs, who sang songs of welcome or puffed down gold leaf and silver foil on the king as he passed beneath.

In 1432 the splendor reached its zenith. The mayor and aldermen realized the unique importance of the occasion—the first coronation of a King of England as King of France too—and were able to plan a long time ahead. They commissioned the poet John Lydgate to commemorate the event in verse, and perhaps to help to plan the elaborate symbolism. The mayor was resplendent in a crimson gown, a great velvet hat trimmed with precious fur, a golden girdle round his waist, and a golden baldrick trailing behind him. The aldermen were dazzling in scarlet and the leading craftsmen were all in white, symbol of the purity of their loyalty, according to Lydgate. The memory of the celebrations for Agincourt was invoked by getting the young king to follow the same route as Henry V had then done, from London Bridge to St. Paul's, via Cornhill and Cheapside, but the *tableaux vivants* were even more numerous and elaborate. They began at London Bridge with a giant who threatened confusion to the king's enemies. At the drawbridge was a tower, draped with silk and cloth-of-arras, out of which emerged three "empresses," clad in velvet, cloth-of-gold, and silk, with golden coronets on their heads. They represented Nature, Grace, and Fortune, and conferred all their gifts on the king in set speeches. They were accompanied on either side by seven white-clad maidens, who presented gifts to the king and sang a roundelay in his honor. After several more allegorical tableaux in Cornhill and Cheapside, the king came to a castle of green jasper, against which stood two great trees bearing the king's arms and ancestry. One line led back to St. Edward and the other to St. Louis of France. At the Little Conduit near St. Paul's was a pageant representing the Trinity, with a multitude of angels singing and playing on various musical instruments. At St. Paul's there was another procession to meet the king, archbishops, and other prelates, and after the service the mayor and leading citizens accompanied the young king to Westminster for a *Te Deum* in Westminster Abbey.

It might take military victories and special coronations to stimulate such elaborate pageantry, but the taste for it was already in such force by Chaucer's time that every year there were processions unconnected with any royal, civic, or guild occasion. The most important of the annual events was the Marching Watch on Midsummer's Eve (June 23) and the Eve of St. Peter and St. Paul (June 28). After sunset on these days bonfires were lit in the

streets and city regulations had to provide for fire precautions. The streets were narrow—often only six to nine
feet wide—and the houses were commonly built of wood;
although city ordinances prescribed roofing with lead,
tiles, or stone, many houses were still roofed with thatch.
Hence regulations repeatedly laid down that in summer
every house was to have a barrel of water in front of it,
and every ward was to have an iron crook to pull down
burning thatch and a good horn to sound the alarm. Door-
ways were decorated with birch, fennel, roses, St. John's
wort, lilies, and other flowers for these summer festivals,
and lanterns were hung at the doors to burn all night. The
wealthier citizens set out tables in front of their doors near
the bonfires, providing meat and drink for their neighbors.

From the Little Conduit near St. Paul's a great procession marched down Cheapside and Cornhill to Aldgate, back again along Fenchurch and Gracechurch streets
to Cornhill, whence it returned to Cheapside and there
broke up. In preparation for this event every alderman
had to choose the most reliable men from the residents in
his ward to form the watch, partly to keep order in the
streets and partly to form the grand procession. We do
not know how many took part in the procession in
Chaucer's day, but by the early sixteenth century there
were about two thousand men. Stow says, "parte of them
being olde Souldiers, of skill to be Captains, Lieutenants,
Sergeants, Corporals, &c., Wiflers, Drommers, and Fifes,
Standard and Ensigne bearers, Sword players, Trumpeters on horsebacke . . . Archers in coates of white fustian
signed on the breast and backe with the armes of the

Cittie . . . there were also divers Pageants, Morris dancers, Constables, the one halfe which was 120 on S. Iohns Eve, the other halfe on S.Peters Eve in bright harnesse, some overgilte, and every one a Iornet [cloak] of Scarlet thereupon, and a chaine of golde, his Hench men following him, his Minstrels before him, and his Cresset light passing by him, the Waytes of the City, the Mayors Officers, for his guard before him, all in a Livery of wolsted or Say Iacquets party coloured, the Mayor himselfe well mounted on horseback, the sword bearer before him in fayre Armour well mounted also, the Mayors footmen & like Torch bearers about him, Hench men twaine, upon great stirring horses following him." Then came the sheriffs' watches. The total number of cresset lights, or pans on long poles, according to Stow, was seven hundred, of which five hundred were provided by the livery companies and two hundred by the city.

In spite of the risk of fire and riot and the expense of mounting the show, these midsummer marching watches were greatly prized. The king and queen, with visitors from abroad, did not disdain to come to watch. They could not be expected to stand among the jostling crowds which thronged the route; by Chaucer's day the royal party had a convenient grandstand attached to the north wall of Bow Church. It had been constructed in the early years of Edward III's reign because of his love of tournaments and of an unfortunate accident that happened in 1329.

Cheapside was a wider street than most of the narrow lanes which formed London's usual thoroughfares and it was a favorite place for tournaments. For such an event the whole length of Cheapside was decorated with bunting and banners, from the church of St. Michael le Querne at the west end to the Stocks Market at the east, but the west end may have been more difficult for jousting because of the Eleanor Cross in the middle of the road, opposite Wood Street. This cross had been erected by Edward I where the body of his beloved first queen had rested on its way from Lincoln to Westminster Abbey; it consisted of a large stone tower, set on a base of steps, surmounted by the Virgin and Child, with representations of the Crucifixion and appropriate saints, such as St. Edward the Confessor. At any rate the tournaments seem to have taken place in the middle of Cheapside opposite the church of St. Mary le Bow. Here young Edward III had a wooden gallery erected from which the ladies of the court could watch the jousts. Unhappily in 1329, just when the young Queen Philippa and some of her ladies had climbed into the gallery, it collapsed; not only were some of the ladies hurt in the fall, but also some of the knights, on whom they descended. The king in his wrath would have severely punished the carpenters responsible for the gallery had not Queen Philippa pleaded for them. To prevent such accidents in future, Edward built against the north wall of the church a stone gallery with a roof. It was called the "crownsilde," or royal pavilion, and was used down to the time of Henry VIII for watching tournaments and the midsummer pageants. The tradition was so strong that when Bow Church had to be rebuilt after the Fire of London, Wren was asked to provide a royal gallery on the north wall of the church, overlooking the street.

The frequent royal visits to London for pageants and for tournaments emphasized the closeness of the connection between the court and the city's ruling class in Chaucer's lifetime. Relationships between the king and London merchants had not been good in the reign of Edward I. In his efforts to increase his income, he tried to encourage the flow of trade, and to this end he protected foreign merchants, going so far as to give alien merchants full rights of London citizenship in 1285. This annoyed the Londoners greatly, and in the strained relationship that followed the autocratic king took the liberties of the city into his hands and kept them for thirteen years. It was only the constitutional crisis of 1297 that forced him to restore the city's self-government. The king's action compelled the small patrician circle that had ruled the city to make common cause with the hitherto despised but increasingly powerful craft guilds, and the ruling Londoners were more determined than before to define the qualifications of citizenship so that aliens would be more clearly excluded.

The troubles of the reign of Edward II gave the city government a chance to do this, and the spirit of unrest which violently threatened the king's conduct of affairs enabled reformers in London to agitate for changes. By the end of the reign the ruling class of London was larger than it had been in Edward I's time, more open to newcomers if they were wealthy and willing to play the game according to accepted rules, and more closely linked with the power and organization of the developing crafts. In 1326 the then mayor became an open partisan of the queen, who was leading a rebellion against her husband in the name of her son, the future Edward III. In 1327, after the deposition of his father, young Edward, in gratitude to the Londoners, issued a new charter confirming various privileges, such as the right of the mayor to act as royal escheator. The policy of co-operation thus begun was intensified three years later, when King Edward needed all the support he could get to overthrow the tyrannous rule of his mother Isabella and her lover Mortimer.

In the 1330's the court spent more time in or near London and more government institutions settled down in London or Westminster. The patronage of a chivalric court, fond of balls and tournaments, fostered the prosperity of those London merchants who were connected with the fine-clothing trades: mercers who supplied silks and linens and accessories like ribbons, drapers who specialized in heavier fabrics, skinners who could provide fashionable and costly furs. The department of the royal household responsible for clothing and liveries, the Great Wardrobe, now settled down in London and purchased stores from London merchants, who thereby became more expert in the buying and selling of luxury goods. The famous Richard Whittington was later to make a good deal of his wealth by supplying velvets, cloth-of-gold, taffetas, and damask, to the Great Wardrobe; in 1392–94 he received nearly £3,500 from this source.

The nobles who thronged the court of Edward III, in the atmosphere of harmony and splendor that now prevailed, soon learned that the fine clothes which presence at court demanded could be bought from the stocks of London merchants. Soon the outbreak of the great war in France increased still further the wealth and prestige of the London merchant class. It is true that Edward made large demands on London. He needed large loans to finance his costly campaigns and alliances, and when he had bankrupted Italian firms like the Bardi and Peruzzi by his failure to repay, he turned to wealthy English subjects, Londoners like Walter Cheriton and Thomas Swanland. These in turn were ruined unless they managed to remain in the background like Henry Picard and John Poultney.

Royal demands necessitated increased taxation and it was moreover necessary to keep the walls in repair in case of French invasion. Indirect taxation like murage proved totally inadequate and wealthier citizens not only had to contribute to direct taxation like tallages but were pressed to make "voluntary" contributions. Nevertheless, even when all this is taken into account, it seems likely that on the whole the London merchant class benefited from the war. The taxation was intermittent and on the whole more onerous on the poor than on the rich, and there was a great deal of money to be made from supplying the armies with clothing and arms.

In spite of aristocratic prejudice to the contrary, wealth brought prestige. There is much evidence that in the declining years of Edward III the wealthier London merchants were considering themselves "gentlemen" and were coming to be taken as such by others. By the late fourteenth century one of the surest touchstones of gentility was the right to display a coat of arms. During the fourteenth century it became common for Londoners of aldermanic rank to bear heraldic arms, so much so that in 1386 a city regulation ordained that the alderman of the ward should prepare a pennon of his arms for the array of the watch. Early in the next century John Carpenter, the Town Clerk, who was probably born near the end of Edward III's reign, wrote in the *Liber Albus* that it was an ancient custom for an alderman to be buried like a baron, with a man on horseback at the funeral displaying the shield, helmet, and other arms of the deceased. Some London merchants may have inherited their arms, but more may have assumed them and asked a painter or seal engraver to design arms to the merchant's taste. A few obtained arms by royal grant. In 1381, Richard II dubbed four merchants knights for their services in ending the Peasants' Revolt. There had never been so many merchant knights dwelling in the city at once, nor were there to be again until Edward IV, who courted the London merchants and made six aldermen knights of the Order of the Bath at his coronation and that of his queen.

The social ambitions of many merchants went further than the use of armorial bearings. They tried to secure the patronage of the nobility and the co-operation of country gentlemen. The register of John of Gaunt records currency transactions with the rich grocers Sir Nicholas Brembre and Sir John Philpot, and the clerk calls them in familiar fashion by their nicknames, "Nichol" and "Jankyn." According to fifteenth-century etiquette books, at formal feasts merchants should be seated at the same table as esquires, though the Mayor of London should be seated with chief judges, barons, and mitered abbots. Noblemen and gentlemen were invited to guild feasts and encouraged to join merchant fraternities. With growing frequency merchants named gentlemen as executors of their wills. To a lesser extent government officials and lawyers reciprocated with London merchants. For example, Thomas Bowes, clerk of the king's ordnance in 1475 and keeper of the royal mint from 1476–79, chose as executor a goldsmith who had held office with him at the mint and bequeathed to him a Bible and his best signet. He left to his son William "£30 to find him to school, and my best primer and psalter book, covered with cloth of gold."

Gentlemen were perhaps more reluctant to intermarry with merchant families, but this did not prevent such matches if there was wealth to be gained. Of the wives of aldermen whose parentage is known, one-fourth were the daughters of country landholders in the fourteenth century and in the following century the proportion rose to one-third. Indeed, by the fifteenth century an alderman who was wealthy, ambitious, and fortunate might marry a peer's daughter, as happened in the case of Geoffrey Boleyn, the great-grandfather of Queen Anne Boleyn. As for the daughters of London merchants, country gentlemen competed for them if they were reputed to have large dowries or if they were widows of rich merchants. Sometimes, indeed, the London family was hesitant about such a match if the bridegroom's family did not have sufficient status. Readers of the Paston Letters will recall that

Geoffrey Boleyn's widow, Lady Anne Boleyn, was not enthusiastic about her youngest daughter's marrying John Paston III. She felt that the girl could do better than that and she is reputed to have commented, "What if he and sche kan agre I will not lette [hinder] it, but I will never advyse hyr thereto in no wyse." But usually both sides saw the advantage of the match, the country gentlemen in terms of wealth, the merchants in terms of prestige. In the fourteenth century about a third of the marriages of aldermen's daughters were to gentlemen and about two-thirds of the remarriages of aldermen's widows.

With good management and good luck it was possible to ascend the social scale in successive remarriages. For example, Matilda Fraunceys, daughter of a mercer who was an alderman from 1352 to 1375, was married first to John Aubrey, a grocer alderman and one of the richest men in London. Matilda's father was wealthy and she probably had a good dowry. John Aubrey died childless in 1380 or 1381, and Matilda was therefore a very desirable match. She married Sir Alan Buxhill, a courtier who did not live long, and then, as her third husband, she married John de Montagu, nephew and heir of the Earl of Salisbury. He succeeded to the title in 1397 and was one of Richard II's most conspicuous adherents, in support of whom he met his death in the rising of 1400. Matilda's brother Adam was more successful in striking roots among the country gentry. He added more to the already considerable London property left by his father, and he bought the rich manor of Cobhams in Essex. He was knighted and settled in the manor of Edmonton which his father had purchased. His daughter Elizabeth married Thomas Charleton, a member of an old Middlesex family, and his son Thomas was also knighted.

The Fr128 — The Frauceys were typical of other prosperous London families, not only in becoming gentry, but in settling down in the home counties. This had the attraction of enabling them to keep one foot in London while they were establishing their position in the country. It also had the advantage that once they had made good their status as country gentlemen they could still, if they wished, keep in touch with London affairs. Landed property gave them social prestige and an assured income; activity as merchants offered chances of rapid advances in wealth. Sir Thomas Bidyk went out to live on the manors of Finchley and Aldermanbury which his citizen father had bought, but his younger son was apprenticed to a mercer and his daughter married a goldsmith. Sir John Philpot, the grocer alderman who was knighted in 1381, acquired property in Kent, near Tonbridge, and his eldest son went to live there. But Sir John's second son was apprenticed to a mercer and his youngest son may have been apprenticed to a goldsmith before he himself founded a family in Kent.

One of the most striking instances of a continued connection with the city is to be met in the Pecche family. John Pecche was a fishmonger who became alderman of Walbrook ward in 1349, sheriff in 1352, and mayor in 1361. He prospered from his trade as a fishmonger and by his marriage to an heiress who brought him properties in London, Middlesex, Surrey, Cambridgeshire, and

Wiltshire. In the 1370's, he was one of the small group of Londoners who became closely associated with John of Gaunt, lending money to the senile Edward III on usurious terms and securing their own profit by monopolies. He was one of those impeached in the Good Parliament of 1376, accused of having purchased a monopoly of the sale of sweet wines in the city and of having used this monopoly to levy a duty on all wine sold, thereby unjustly raising its price. His foes in the city deprived him not only of the aldermanship, but of the franchise as well. Nevertheless, he was not ruined nor did his family become estranged from the city. He had bought the manor of Lullingstone in Kent from the Rokesles and his son Sir William went to live there. But his grandson John, who was also knighted, joined the Drapers' Company in 1427–28; and John's son, Sir William, was admitted to the Grocers' Company in 1459.

John Pecche was by no means exceptional in trying to make money out of royal service. He may have overreached himself and been unlucky as well, but royal service contributed to the fortunes of many London merchants. Sometimes they were able to supply not only clothing but food and other commodities to the royal household. Apart from payment they might be given some place in the royal household, such as yeoman or esquire, which did not require court attendance but entitled them to the rank of gentleman. This is one explanation of the fact that, after an act of 1415 had required a man's occupation or status to be defined in various classes of legal documents, quite a sprinkling of London merchants were officially described as "gentlemen."

Merchants were also used in the royal service at the royal mint, as customs collectors, as king's butler, and as tax collectors. Sometimes the office was a royal one within the city itself. Richard Whittington was appointed collector of the wool custom and subsidy in London from 1401–1403 and 1407–10. This appointment could help both his profits as a merchant and his activities as a great lender to the Crown. He could ensure that his licenses to export wool without paying customs duty would be obeyed without question and he could see that assignments made on the customs of London for repayment of his loans were given first priority. This was important to him, for he was a great lender both to Richard II and to the first two Lancastrian kings; there are only two years between 1400 and his death in 1423 when Whittington did not lend money to the king.

In view of the close connections between London merchants and the royal household, it is not surprising that Geoffrey Chaucer, son of a London merchant who had held a royal office, should have taken service in the household of Lionel Duke of Clarence, that he should have married one of Queen Philippa's ladies-in-waiting, and that he himself in 1367 should have been made an esquire of the king's chamber. Nor it it strange that a century later William Caxton, as a leading mercer, should have found fairly easy entry to court circles in his quest for business, and should have gained patronage from courtiers like Earl Rivers and the Earl of Arundel.

Merchants with such social aspirations and high social contacts naturally wanted a good education for their children. It might seem at first that the number of schools in fourteenth-century London was very meager. There were only three recognized grammar schools in the city: St. Paul's, St. Martin-le-Grand, and Bow Church. But there seems to have been an increasing demand for education, and in 1393 the Bishop of London ordered several rivals to desist on the ground that they were conducting "general schools of grammar" without being properly qualified. Grammar schools were regarded as of special importance, for an education there might lead on to the university and preferment in the Church, and consequently the Bishop of London and the Chancellor of St. Paul's were cautious about licensing such schools, especially as they might be jealous of rivals.

Of the three ancient grammar schools, St. Paul's seems to have been the best. We do not know whether Chaucer attended this school, but what is certain is that the library of this school contained almost everything that his poems show him to have read in his youth. It was especially rich in classical and post-classical authors; and it had the remarkable provision in its rules that graduates of the school could borrow books from the library provided that they guaranteed to return them. In the next century the growing demand for education burst the official monopoly of St. Paul's and its two sister schools, and by the 1430's two new schools had been founded at St. Dunstan's in the East and at St. Anthony's Hospital. In 1447 four new grammar schools were established (by act of Parliament, perhaps to circumvent the Bishop of London) in the parishes of All Hallows the Great, St. Andrew Holborn, St. Peter Cornhill, and St. Mary Colechurch for St. Thomas of Acon Hospital. Of these the most famous was that of St. Anthony's Hospital. Stow tells us that the rivalry between St. Paul's School and St. Anthony's was great enough to induce their boys to fight in the street and hit each other with their satchels of books. The St. Anthony's boys called those of St. Paul's "pigeons" because so many pigeons were bred at St. Paul's, and the St. Paul's boys taunted their rivals as "pigs" because St. Anthony was commonly pictured followed by a pig and because St. Anthony's Hospital was the only institution in London allowed to own pigs. (They roamed the streets and wore bells to identify them and to attract attention; it was an act of charity to feed them, for in that way one was helping the hospital.)

The reputation of St. Anthony's School belonged to a later age than that of Chaucer, but educational facilities in fourteenth-century London were not limited to three schools. Even before the official approval of new grammar schools in the fifteenth century, unofficial ones apparently existed. In the early fifteenth century John Seward, who has survived in memory as the prolific writer of Latin verse and educational works, was a grammar-school master in Cornhill. He was a member of a literary circle in London which, from the evidence of his writings, included a Master William Relyk who taught grammar at a school held in the Cardinal's Hat tavern in Lombard Street. Yet neither of these schools was official, and if this happened in the reigns of Henry IV and Henry V, there is no reason why it should not have occurred under Richard II.

There were also a number of less pretentious schools, both elementary and commercial. Parish and chantry priests were sometimes willing to give simple instruction free of charge. If one was able to pay, there was a choice not only of teachers in London, but of others elsewhere. In 1374 Robert Brynkle, a mercer of London, was committed to prison by the Mayor's Court for not rendering an account of a sum of £300 entrusted to him to trade on behalf of Thomas, son and heir of Hugh atte Boure, late mercer, and also for having taken Thomas as an apprentice during his wardship without the permission of the court. Three months later Brynkle rendered account, showing that he had paid net interest of 10 per cent on the loan; he had increased the original sum substantially and yet had also educated the boy for ten years at Oxford. The cost of the lad's board at Oxford had been 104s a year, 40s for his clothing, and 26s/8d for his teaching. This was more than the annual cost of educating a London grocer's son at Croydon in 1394. The price of board and lodging was the same—2s a day—but the Croydon schoolmaster's salary was only 13s/4d a year. Doubtless the Oxford school had greater prestige. Most Londoners in their teens, if they were receiving formal education, probably acquired it in London itself. If they were not attending a grammar school, they could have been sent to a commercial school run by a scrivener. In a manual of commercial French composed about 1415, a twelve-year-old boy is made to declare that he has attended the school of

William Kyngesmyll, where in a short time he has been taught to read, to write, to cast accounts, and to speak French, so that he is now ready to be apprenticed.

Often, however, education was provided during the apprenticeship. Sometimes this led to disputes, as a number of cases in Chancery bear witness. In one of them, about 1451, the petitioner, Thomas Bodyn, complained that when he was apprenticed for twelve years, at the age of fourteen, to Robert Chirche, haberdasher, it was agreed that for the first one and one-half years he should be taught grammar and for the next six months instructed in writing. But Chirche had failed to carry out this pledge, though eight years of the apprenticeship had now elapsed.

Sometimes the education provided savored of the methods of Mr. Squeers in *Nicholas Nickleby*. We have already met the allegation that Thomas Grene had been driven to a mental breakdown by being compelled to perform menial services. Another Chancery petition, about 1450, shows that apprentices could be sensitive to the claims of social status in their education. William Elmeshall, an apprentice to Thomas Batter, draper, had run away because, it was said, Batter had sent him for his two years' schooling to a priest who "set him in his kitchen to wash pots, pans, dishes and to dress meat." But an earlier part of his indenture had stipulated that he should not "carry water pots nor do any defiling labour, but only attend upon his school and on learning his craft." As, however, he had been degraded in this manner, he had run away. These cases show that masters could abuse their trust for the education of their apprentices. Yet the very fact that it was possible to bring complaints to Chancery and to the Mayor's Court in London, and that action was taken on these complaints, shows that public opinion was alert to the injustice of such abuses and tried to stop them.

We naturally tend to hear more of the cases where the arrangement failed than those where it succeeded. London was still small enough and its governing class still sufficiently local and cohesive to have a policy in such matters. The best testimony that policy in favor of education was effective is the increase of literacy in London. From the evidence of the proofs of literacy or illiteracy in the consistory court of London in the next century it has been calculated that by the reign of Edward IV some 40 per cent of male Londoners could read Latin. It is likely that in Chaucer's time the proportion was less than this, but more lay Londoners are likely to have been able to read English than to understand Latin. In 1422 the brewers of London decided to keep their records in English for "there are many of our craft of brewers who have the knowledge of writing and reading in the said English idiom," whereas few of them could read Latin. As yet the poorer members of the crafts were often illiterate. The heresy trials in the reigns of Henry IV and Henry V show that in the study circles formed by Lollards—mostly composed, so far as laymen were concerned, of lesser craftsmen and journeymen—one man would read to the rest of the company such Lollard tracts as *The Wycket* and *The Lantern of Light*, written in English.

The business concerns of merchants were clearly being conducted on a basis of written records and accounting, so that in a merchant's office ability to read, write, and cast accounts must have been required for employment. For the merchants themselves literacy was not always confined to what was needed to conduct the business; some of them began to own a few books. Sir William Walworth specified ten in his will, mostly religious works, with an emphasis on biblical studies. Apart from a Bible and the Epistles of St. Paul, he bequeathed to the Austin friars a "lyre," (probably the biblical commentaries of Nicholas of Lyra, c. 1270–1340) and to the Carthusians of Smithfield a *Hugutio* (probably his Book of Derivations). In these and a "legend," or book of saints' lives, he was typical of other merchants. Bequests of this period and of the early fifteenth century from London merchants are mainly of missals, primers, legends, books of the Bible, devotional works, and grammars. Sometimes a philosophical work like Boethius' *Consolations of Philosophy* or historical works like the *Brut* or Higden's *Polychronicon* will appear. The *Polychronicon* gave them a view of world history as it was then understood. The *Brut* satisfied their interest in the early (and largely mythical) story of Britain. It offered a basis on which to build a history of their city, of which Londoners had already been proud when FitzStephen wrote in the twelfth century. For Chaucer's contemporaries London's recent history was worth recording in continuations of the *Brut* chronicle.

The number of books named as having belonged to London merchants in Chaucer's day is meager. We have learned to realize, however, that wills were not exhaustive statements of chattels owned by the deceased, but were only those which were valued or available for disposal. Moreover, the range of reading may have been increased by borrowing. Chaucer not only had frequent dealings with great merchants like Sir William Walworth, Sir Nicholas Brembre, Sir John Philpot, but also with knights and officials of various kinds: Sir William Beauchamp, Sir Guichard d'Angle, Sir John Burley, Sir Peter Courtenay, Sir Lewis Clifford, Sir William Neville, Sir John Clanvowe, and Sir Richard Sturry. Some of these, like Sir Guichard d'Angle, tutor to Richard II, and Sir Peter Courtenay, king's chamberlain, could have strengthened his contacts with the royal court and its culture; some like Sir John Clanvowe, author of a devotional treatise *The Two Ways*, were writers themselves. It is possible that Chaucer was able to borrow books from these friends, and what Chaucer could do may have been possible for other Londoners from the merchant class.

There were also a growing number of libraries in London. We have seen that St. Paul's School had a valuable library available to its graduates. A library was built up at the Guildhall as merchants left bequests to it; John Carpenter, the Common Clerk, left a large number of volumes, for example. As wealth grew and literacy spread, merchants were leaving books to parish churches. In 1368, a mercer bequeathed to St. Lawrence Jewry a Bible, a missal, a book of saints' lives, and a portable breviary. There were also libraries attached to the religious houses and hospitals. Richard Whittington gave £400 for the building of the Greyfriars' library as well as leaving money which was in part devoted to the building of the Guildhall library.

Soon there were enough customers to support a commercial lending library. John Shirley, who died in 1456, had a large house and four shops, rented from St. Bartholomew's Hospital, and seems to have done a considerable trade in lending manuscripts, usually in English, of authors like Chaucer and Lydgate, books of devotion, and books on hunting like the *Master of Game*, by the second Duke of York. Even by 1403 there were so many producers of books in London that they petitioned the king to be allowed to elect annually two wardens to supervise the work of text writers, illuminators, and bookbinders, to present to the mayor and aldermen those accused of bad workmanship, and to have power to call together the members of the craft to make bylaws.

Merchants who could provide a careful education for their children, take an interest in books written in English, and have close contacts with the court and the nobility were likely to want fine houses for themselves. We saw in Chapter I that some of these houses were so impressive that they were taken over by princes or nobles. For visitors the exteriors of such houses added distinction to the face of London. Those persons who gained admission to the interior would find some pretensions to comfort and dignity. Even at the beginning of the fourteenth century the not specially remarkable house of the skinner William de Hanigtone, contracted for him in 1308 by Simon de Canterbury, contained a number of rooms. It was to have a hall with a bay window at the dais end, a room with a chimney, and a larder between them. There was to be a sun parlor over the sitting room and larder. At the top end of the hall there was to be a bay window and the door of the hall was to be protected from drafts by a porch. Beneath the hall were to be two cellars and a "sewer" next to them. Next to the hall, and by an old kitchen that already stood on the site, was to be a stable, with another sun parlor above the stable and a garret room above that. At one end of the sun parlor was to be a kitchen with a fireplace and between the hall and "the old chamber" was to be a room, eight feet wide, with a bay window.

Such a merchant could entertain, and be entertained by, the more affluent clergy of London, such as the canons of St. Paul's. We find, for example, in the will of Thomas Warde, canon of St. Paul's who died in 1452, that besides being able to leave a good many bequests in money and vestments of costly materials and workmanship, he had possessed some attractive household furnishings. Among these were the fine bedclothes and hangings that had adorned the bed in his great chamber, the worsted furnishings of another bed (presumably in another room), and the furnishings of his best bed. The latter were of green arras, worked with three images of girls, and included a featherbed and a pair of fustian blankets. He also had some attractive silver cups and saltcellars with which to entertain his friends. His soft furnishings all bore his motto, *Fiat voluntas Dei*.

Lesser men were not without a range of useful furnishings. In 1337, Hugh le Bevere, probably a tavern owner, was accused of murdering his wife, and as he refused to plead, he was committed to Newgate, "there in penance to remain until he should be dead." His goods and chattels were confiscated by the sheriffs of London. The inventory cannot be complete for it lacks any beds or women's clothes. Perhaps these were claimed by the wife's family. Even so, the list is impressive for an ordinary taverner. The bedding included a mattress, three featherbeds, two pillows, six blankets, seven sheets, a coverlet, and a green tapestry. There were six chests, two chairs, one folding table, five cushions, a best tablecloth worth 2s, three working tablecloths valued at 6d each, and two curtains. The kitchen was well supplied with seven brass cooking pots, a spit, a frying pan, a tripod, two basins, a washing bowl, and two tubs. (This man had evidently shared in the rise in the standard of living of fourteenth-century London whereby the more affluent replaced earthenware kitchen utensils with metal ones.) Le Bevere also possessed a nut cup with a foot and cover of silver valued at 30s, six silver spoons worth 6s, and a mazer cup priced at 6s. The list of clothing is also incomplete, but at any rate he possessed three fine robes lined with fur, one worsted gown and overcoat, two other gowns, two other overcoats, and two hoods. For service in the city militia he also had a hackton, or stuffed leather jacket, and a helmet. There is no mention of small household implements such as knives or spoons or of usual furniture such as benches, yet this incomplete list was valued at £15/2/4d. This is a considerable sum in view of the fact that

William de Hanigtone's entire house was to cost about the same amount.

The trade carried on by Hugh le Bevere seems to be identified by the six casks of wine, each valued at one mark (13/4d). Six years earlier it had been decreed that a gallon of best Gascon wine should sell for 4d and a gallon of best Rhenish wine for 8d. So even if Hugh's wine was the best Rhenish, he would have had 120 gallons, and if it was best Gascon or Bordeaux he would have had 240 gallons. If it was inferior wine, he would have been holding even larger quantities. The price would depend on an assurance that it was not more than a year old. Until better methods of rendering barrels airtight or of keeping wine in tightly corked glass bottles were invented in the eighteenth century, it was almost impossible to prevent wine from turning into vinegar within two or three years. Hence the value set on having wines that were not only new but strong; delicate wines were not prized because they would not keep.

The first wines to arrive after the harvest, about November, were known as wines of vintage, but the most prized were wines of rack, which were racked off their lees in spring and shipped to England in April, May, and June. Most of the wine drunk in England came from Gascony and other parts of France. German, Italian, Spanish, Portuguese, and Cyprus wines were more expensive because more difficult to transport, but sweet wines like vernage, osey, romeny, and malmsey were greatly prized as a contrast to the acidity of much of the other wine.

As the wine ships sailed under London Bridge a toll of 2d was levied on every cask for the repair of the bridge. As wines were often harsh and sour, it was a very common practice to blend them with spices, honey, and herbs to disguise the taste. They were then called piments, clarry, or hippocras. This custom of blending wines opened the door to fraud; old or inferior wines might be mixed in. One device was to put the dregs of all wines into a cask lined with cobbler's wax or pitch, which gave it the color and something of the flavor of romeny, by which name it was sold. Such malpractices were constantly sought for and publicly punished if discovered. In 1364 John Rightwys and John Penrose, vintners, were presented to the mayor and aldermen by the supervisors of wines in the city for selling red wine which was "unsound and unwholesome for man." Rightwys was acquitted, but Penrose was found guilty and condemned to drink a draught of the same wine that he had sold to customers. The rest of the wine was then poured over his head, and he was to forswear the trade of vintner in the city forever. However, he had influence, and just over four years later he was readmitted to trade in London.

Wine was usually sold in a tavern (in the above case, the tavern of Walter Doget in East Cheap). Because of the risk of fraud, an order was made that sweet wines should not be kept in the same cellar with other wines. When this was found to be unworkable, an ordinance was made in 1365 that sweet wines should not be sold anywhere except in three taverns set aside for the purpose, in Walbrook, Lombard Street, and Cheapside. This was supposed to keep the sale of sweet wines under official control. In 1365 they were let to Richard Lyons, the notorious vintner, for ten years at £200 a year, a sum which was to be devoted to the repair of the city walls and the cleaning of the ditches. In 1376, Lyons was impeached, his monopoly was canceled, and his stocks of wine at the taverns were confiscated. Thereafter sweet wines were sold in ordinary taverns.

The badge of a tavern was either a hoop (to remind the customer of a barrel) or an alestake with a bunch of leaves or "bush" fastened to it. The particular tavern was then distinguished by a brightly painted sign. Names that occur in fourteenth-century city records include The Cock, The Red Door, The Goat, The Bell, The Star, The Cat and Fiddle, The Lion at the Door, The Moon, and The Sun. Some of the taverns or inns were fine enough to be meeting places of leading guilds until they built their own halls. The first Salters' Hall was erected about 1454 and in 1477 the Salters wished to extend it. They therefore bought an adjacent inn, The George on the Hoop, which had no fewer than thirty-two beds and extensive stables, with a cellar convenient for drinking.

The imports of wine were so large that the capacity of ships was measured by "tonnage" or the number of "tuns" that they could carry. A whole ward of the city by the Thames, near the wharves on the west side of Dowgate at the mouth of the Walbrook, about Queenhithe, was known as the Vintry from the large number of wine merchants who dwelled there. Between 1377 and 1394 vintners were the sixth most numerous group of aldermen

(28), being outnumbered only by grocers (108), mercers (85), fishmongers (58), goldsmiths (44), and drapers (35). Chaucer would have been familiar with questions on regulations of the wine trade through his father's activities. In 1342, for example, John Chaucer was present with fourteen other vintners to consent to an ordinance made by the mayor and aldermen for preventing the sale of bad wine in taverns. In 1347 he was made deputy in the port of Southampton to the king's chief butler, a post he held for over two years. John Chaucer's duties would have included not only those of exacting the king's prisage of wine from every ship, but also of seeing that civic regulations were obeyed. In his son's later years the civic authorities were much worried over the price of wine, for the insecurity of the seas in the later fourteenth century enhanced the price of imported drinks. Capture of a wine fleet, such as the Earl of Arundel achieved in 1387, or an exceptionally good vintage, as in 1394, could bring down the price of wine for a time. But wine normally cost three to five times what it had a century earlier.

It was generally agreed that towns must regulate strictly the conduct of trade within their jurisdiction, especially trade in drink and foodstuffs, and this view was fully maintained in London. All imported goods had to be sold within forty days and were to be disposed of openly where they were landed or at the "seld" where they were stored, not by private sale. Salt, so essential for flavoring and for preserving food, was imported in large quantities from the Bay of Bourgneuf on the coast of Poitou. This "Bay" salt had to be measured and carted from the landing wharves on a fixed scale of charges by officials known as "salt meters." Imported leather had to be sold at a "seld" in Friday Street; imported cloth, from 1387, at the Stocks Market, and from 1396 at Bakewell Hall, near the Guildhall, which the mayor and commonalty had bought from the Banquell family and then used for a weekly cloth market.

There was a very strong notion that there should be a recognized price for commodities, based on custom, and any attempt to exceed this price, either because of scarcity or, worse, because of any attempt to corner the market, must be sternly and swiftly suppressed. In 1375, for example, Mayor William Walworth was walking among the poulterers at St. Nicholas Shambles to see at what price poultry was being sold. He asked John Andrew, a poulterer, the price of a goose and Andrew told him 8d or 7d, whereupon the mayor ordered him to charge no more than 6d. Andrew answered that he would not bring any geese to the city for forty days. The mayor at once committed him to prison, and, three days later, when he was brought before the mayor and aldermen, he was told not to buy, sell, or bring any poultry within the liberties of the city for seven weeks on pain of the pillory. In 1382, Thomas Welford, a fishmonger, brought in a shipload of salted herrings to Queenhithe and sold them at five for a penny to the retailers, who therefore could not afford to sell them to the customers for less than four for a penny. Complaint was made to the mayor and aldermen, who at once interviewed Welford and, with much difficulty, got him to agree to sell to the retailers at six for a penny. This was on a Saturday. On the following Monday Welford sold some of his herrings at the rate of ten for a penny to a stranger, William Botild, to carry out of the city for sale. When the mayor and aldermen heard of this transaction, they were very angry, since it was a well-known rule that all freemen should sell to fellow Londoners as cheaply as they sold to strangers, if not cheaper. On Tuesday the mayor and aldermen therefore decided that Welford and other erring fishmongers should sell their herrings at nine for a penny.

It was not only traders who were controlled by the city in this way. Workmen were also subjected to civic supervision. For example, in November, 1349, when the plague had made labor scarce, a number of cordwainers complained to the mayor that their servants had conspired to strike unless their wages were raised. The mayor and aldermen committed the offending workmen to Newgate until they had promised to work for the same wages as before. In 1381 it was discovered that a regular organization of journeymen spurriers had been meeting for nine years in a garden and had officials and a common fund. Members swore to keep up their piece rates for work done, to allow only journeymen to belong to their society, to refuse to do work for strangers, and so on. The mayor and aldermen indicted all the leading members in the Chamber of the Guildhall and made them promise to end such a conspiracy for all time to come and to distribute the common funds to their poorer members.

Traders in foodstuffs were especially watched, and a favorite punishment was to set the offender in the pillory.

If the offense was that of selling bad meat (and meat was hard to keep fresh in hot weather), a favorite penalty was to burn the putrid beef or poultry under the nose of the pilloried victim. In 1382, for example, John Welburgham was not only made to repay sixpence to complainants to whom he had sold rotten conger eel, but was put in the pillory and the stinking fish was burned before him. If it was unsound wine, a corresponding penalty might be imposed, as we have seen in the case of Rightwys and Penrose in 1364.

Since by Chaucer's time wine had increased greatly in cost in relation to ale, most of the time Londoners drank more ale than wine. The city was already renowned for its ale, which was brewed in vast quantities. In 1309 the city was said to contain 354 taverns and 1,334 breweries. In 1391 there is a reference in the Letter Books to "hoppyngbeer." If this is beer with hops, it cannot have been widely used, for hops would have been a good preservative and one of the great problems with ale at this time was the fact that it would not keep for more than a few weeks, especially in summer heat. It was very annoying to have to throw it away because it had gone flat, so alehouses and inns were constantly tempted to sell ale that was too old or, if need be, to add such spices as pepper to disguise the bad taste.

Aletasters or "ale conners" were appointed in London, two to four in each ward. They were supposed to be called in by a brewer each time he brewed, and they had the right to sample the drink in alehouses. Through the aldermen, the offenders were indicted at the Guildhall, the usual punishment being the pillory. Offenses included the use of fraudulent measures and the charging of too high a price. For example, in 1337 the mayor and aldermen ordained that a gallon of the best ale should cost not more than three halfpence, a gallon of medium ale not more than a penny, and ale of poorer quality not more than three farthings. Evidently there had been much trouble on this point recently, for instead of punishment in the pillory, convicted offenders were to be imprisoned three days and fined forty pence for the first offense, and for the third offense to be banished from the city. It was important that the city government should prevent abuses in such a matter, for the king was interested in obtaining ale from London for the royal household, sometimes buying and sometimes requisitioning. Londoners were so used to this that in 1394 an imposter, John Haselwode, managed to collect a good deal of money from people to save them from such requisitioning before he was caught and sentenced.

Offenders in the brewing and selling of ale were often women, for ale brewing and alehouse keeping was a typically female occupation. Mistress Nell Quickly was as typical of Chaucer's London as Falstaff's. We do not hear of a Master Quickly and there is no reason why Mistress Quickly should not have acted as hostess of the Boar's Head on her own. Girls were brought up to view marriage as a normal stage in their lives (unless they became nuns), but there are many instances of married women having employees, even apprentices, and carrying on one business (especially tavern keeping) while their husbands conducted another trade. Moreover, a woman could continue her husband's business when she became a widow and enjoy the privileges of a freewoman of the city, though she was likely to be soon snapped up by a second husband—especially if she were keeping a comfortable and lucrative inn.

Taverns varied greatly in social esteem. Some of them, as we have seen, were good enough to attract the meetings of leading guildsmen, or even of the mayor and aldermen. Even in Southwark, which had a dubious reputation in general, the Walnut Tree and the Tabard Inn, where Chaucer's pilgrims met, were regarded as very respectable, whereas some inns in Southwark and Cock Lane Smithfield, like the Saracen's Head, Swan, Boar's Head, and Cross Keys were notorious as brothels. One cannot imagine the mayor and aldermen meeting at the tavern described in *Piers Plowman*, frequented by a seamstress, a rabbit catcher, a tinker and his apprentices, a hackney man and a huckster, or peddler, a whore and the parish clerk, a parson and his mistress, a ditcher, a fiddler, a rat catcher, a Cheapside crossing sweeper, a ropemaker, a road man, a dishwasher, a cobbler, and a butcher's girl—all drinking so long and hard that one of them vomited on his neighbor.

But for the poor the taverns undoubtedly formed an important meeting place, a warm refuge from their crowded, flimsy, drafty houses. Except for the diversions of a Prince Hal, the great of the land did not need taverns. An earl of March or Suffolk, a bishop of Ely or of Hereford, an abbot of Bury or of Ramsey might frequent a spacious inn in which he and his friends and servants could not only feast and drink, but find many other amusements—dancing, gaming, listening to traveling minstrels and poets like Chaucer reading their works, playing draughts, chess, and round games like blind man's buff—but for other diversions the great either went to another great house, including the royal court, or, in spring and summer, flocked out of doors.

In and around London the great could indulge in various outdoor amusements: hunting and hawking in the woods and marshes, tournaments in Cheapside, at Smithfield, or at Westminster, and water sports on the river. Lesser folk also found amusement out of doors when the weather permitted. In winter there was skating, tobogganing, and sliding, especially on the wide sheets of ice on Moor Fields. Shrove Tuesday was the great day for cockfighting and football, and schools rivaled each other in these activities. At Easter there were contests on the water; a shield was hung on a pole, fixed in midstream, and from boats, carried along by the current, young men standing in them tried to break lances against the shield. If, as often happened, they fell into the water, they had to be fished out quickly, and the crowds of bystanders on the banks laughed and clapped. On May Day there were outdoor games and shows, and maypoles were set up. The most noted was that before the south door of St. Andrew's in Aldgate Street, which thereby acquired its name of St. Andrew Undershaft and kept its famous maypole until the Puritans destroyed it during the Commonwealth.

The long warm days of summer naturally gave the

greatest opportunities for outdoor activities. There were the processions and tournaments already mentioned, and sometimes there were open-air plays. In 1391 the parish clerks of London presented a play for three days at the skinners' well by Smithfield, at which the king, queen, and court were present, and in 1409 a miracle play was acted for eight days. In summer there were quintain contests especially on Cornhill by the Standard. A freely swiveling horizontal bar was set on top of an upright post and at either end of the bar was hung a bag of sand and a broad shield. Contestants rode hard at the shield; if they missed, they were scorned, and if they hit it, they had to ride all the faster to avoid being hit on the neck and perhaps thrown off their horses by the bag of sand swinging round. After evensong and on holy days in summer youths competed in leaping, dancing, shooting, wrestling, throwing of balls or stones. If there was time to go farther, citizens could walk over the moorfields to the north of the city and, if they had the energy, venture as far as Islington, Hoxton, or Bethnal Green. If they wanted coarser entertainment, they could go to Southwark. There, in addition to the brothels and doubtful taverns, were bear gardens, where they could watch bears baited by mastiffs; bull-rings, where dogs were tossed high in the air by maddened bulls and caught on sticks so that their fall was broken, while the bulls were being savaged to death by other dogs; cockpits, where cocks armed with spurs would strike furiously at each other and strew the sandpit with blood and feathers; and fighting booths, where men slashed at each other with swords to entertain the roaring onlookers.

As the days drew shorter, the entertainments had to be nearer home. At Martinmas (November 10) there were bonfires in the streets, with roasting of pigs and oxen by neighbors who clubbed together for this festivity, but thereafter most of the amusements had to be back indoors again. For the poor it had to be self-made diversions, like singing, talking, and dicing over a pot of cheap ale in a mean tavern. They might be given the privilege of being allowed as spectators and receivers of food doles in a great house or even the king's court at Christmas, when there was not only feasting but entertainments presided over by a lord of misrule. These entertainments included mumming, which involved dressing up and wearing masks, acting plays in the manner of charades, and then feasting and dancing. In 1377 the citizens of London organized an impressive mumming for the young King Richard, then at Kennington with his mother, the Duke of Lancaster, and other nobles. Accompanied by minstrels with trumpets, sackbuts, cornets, and shawms, with innumerable torchlights made of wax (and therefore very costly), 130 masked citizens rode from Newgate through Cheapside over the bridge to Southwark and thence to Kennington. They were dressed as esquires, knights, cardinals, envoys, pope, and emperor. When they reached the hall, they played dice with the young king, arranging for him to win each time. Then they were feasted and this was followed by dancing and drinking.

This brief account of games and pastimes would be misleading if it gave the impression that Londoners were able to spend their lives in pleasure seeking. In reality most Londoners had to work hard and the working hours were long. In 1394 the blacksmiths asked the mayor and aldermen to confirm some ordinances in which it was laid down that because of possible disturbance of neighbors blacksmiths were not to start work until 6:00 A.M. between November 1 and February 1, and not before daybreak for the rest of the year. Except between November 1 and February 1, when the closing hour was 8:00 P.M., they could carry on work until 9:00 P.M. Six in the morning to eight or nine at night seems to have been normal for most trades; all victualers and taverners kept to these times. Since apprentices lived with masters and family businesses were the rule, shops could open at this hour, and as the appropriate craft processes were usually carried on in a room behind the shop, apprentices and journeymen could be kept busy right from 6:00 A.M. Indeed, Londoners had to be restrained from shopping before 6:00 A.M. In 1354 they were ordered not to buy corn before prime, which was probably 6:00 A.M., and the same rule was applied to the fishmarket in 1360. To make sure that no fish was sold before this time, it was specified that the hour of prime had to be sounded by the bells of St. Paul's before trading could begin. Similarly, there were repeated ordinances forbidding evening markets, usually on the grounds of the risk of fraud if people could not see what they were buying.

In 1328 the mayor and aldermen sent gifts to the

young King Edward and Queen Philippa. To the king they sent ten carcasses of beef, twenty pigs, twenty-four swans, twenty-four bitterns and herons, ten dozen capons, four barrels of pickled sturgeon, six of pike, and six of eels. To the queen they sent five carcasses of beef, twelve pigs, twelve swans, two barrels of sturgeon, three of pike, three of eels, and twelve pheasants. All these, together with eight stones of wax, cost nearly £100. But though there might be a variety of food for the people at the top of society, those at the bottom had to put up with a monotonous diet. The cookshops advertised a great variety of meats, including poultry, but for the poor wheaten bread was too dear to buy and meat was a rarity. They were much addicted by necessity to a potage of vegetables—peas, beans, and cabbage—washed down by cheap ale. And persons without influence were especially likely to be the victims of the cheating which, according to the recorded indictments, seems to have been a constant feature of the sale of food. Bread was sold light in weight, of bad quality, or at a higher price than it should have been, in spite of city regulations. In 1327 ten bakers (eight men and two women) were condemned by the mayor and aldermen of having had molding boards with holes in the middle in their bakehouses; when customers placed dough on the board, someone underneath stole pieces of dough through the hole. The guilty persons were condemned to stand in the pillory with dough hung around their necks. As for meat and fish, they were often sold when they were going putrid, and dodges were used to disguise the condition, such as putting the meat in a pastry and warming it up or drenching it in spices such as pepper. Again, offenders were usually shamed by exposure in the pillory, but judging by the frequency with which such offenses continued, the temptation to make money in this way was greater than the fear of exposure.

If the poor should contract food poisoning through eating bad food, it was difficult for them to get proper medical care or nursing. Even if they escaped the attentions of imposters like Roger Clerk, mentioned earlier, they might fall into the hands of men claiming to be surgeons and knowing nothing about the craft, as we are told in a petition to the mayor and aldermen in 1376. The genuine physicians and barber-surgeons had a mixture of skill, traditional lore, and astrology, and might or might not provide a remedy; but famous physicians like John Gaddesdon and well-known surgeons like Arderne, who were making advances in their subjects in Edward III's reign, were far too expensive for ordinary folk.

Physicians and surgeons might well be needed, too, because of the violence of life. Every man carried a weapon (unless he was in holy orders, and even they did not always ensure that a man was weaponless). There was no strong social convention, as nowadays, that respectable persons should refrain from striking each other, however strong the provocation, and armed brawls were always occurring in the streets of the city. The presence of the mayor and aldermen was no guarantee against violence, though their dignity caused a serious view to be taken of such an occurrence. In 1373, John Lightfoot, salter, did not dare to stir out of the house of Thomas de Mordone, chandler, near Billingsgate, for fear of assault, so the mayor was informed and arrived to keep the peace. He arrested Robert Brabazon, a fishmonger who was apparently lying in wait for Lightfoot, to whom the mayor offered a safe conduct. Then Brabazon, now under arrest, tried to stab Lightfoot with a dagger in the mayor's presence, for which he was committed to Newgate prison for a year and a day.

But assault does not seem to have carried much, if any, social stigma. In 1365 certain fishmongers instigated a murderous attack on a fellow fishmonger, Giles Pykeman, in Bridge Street. Among these instigators was Nicholas Exton, who was afterward mayor in 1386 and 1387. Street fights took place every year between trade rivals, especially the apprentices: between saddlers and lorimers, spicers and pepperers, tailors and drapers. Londoners were suspicious of strangers, so that there were brawls between London workmen and country workmen ready to labor for lower pay, and between Londoners and traders from overseas. Flemings and Italians were constantly apprehensive about the risk of assault, with good reason, and the Hanseatic merchants found it prudent to keep behind the high walls of the Steelyard as much as possible, especially at night. The rich and influential were to some extent able to protect themselves against these violent attacks, if not immediately, then by tracking down the offenders afterward. But those without position or influence often succumbed to robbery and wounding or death.

This last observation may give a gloomy picture of life

in Chaucer's London, but we must retain a sense of balance. If London was a place of dirt and violence, it was also a city which had not yet lost a sense of community. It is significant that loneliness does not seem to have been a social problem, as it is in a modern city, nor was there such a segregation of social classes and occupations. Nearly every regularly employed worker knew his employer personally, lived in the same neighborhood, often in the same street or even the same house, attended the same church, shopped at the same stalls, watched the same processions and amusements. If there was resentment, it was resentment against known individuals, not against a faceless class or the general structure and tone of society. If there was warmth of emotion, it was not for general social causes or world humanitarian efforts, but affection for one's family, for one's neighbors and parish—and for London. As Chaucer walked the London streets, whether as a member of the royal household, as controller in the port of London, as clerk of the king's works, or simply as a resident above Aldgate, he would have met plenty of people he knew. He would have encountered all sorts and conditions of men, from bishops and earls to crossing sweepers and porters. He would have witnessed a noisy and animated scene, dirty and disorderly perhaps, but prosperous, proud of itself, and full of life not yet dispersed to distant suburbs. The city's proclamation of November, 1326, during the rebellion against Edward II, described London as "a mirror to all England." As Chaucer pushed through the bustling shopping crowds in Cheapside and Cornhill on his way back to his house over the gate, he may well have met the originals of Troilus or Criseyde, Pandarus or Diomede, the prioress or the wife of Bath, the merchant or the serjeant-at-law, the physician or the summoner, or the host himself, Harry Bailey— "a fairer burgeys is there noon in Chepe." London had enough variety, importance, and cohesion to have encompassed them all.

Selected Bibliography

Though there remain many questions about life in four-teenth-century London which cannot be answered for lack of information, London is fortunate in having, preserved in the Corporation of London Records Office behind Guildhall, far more available records for that period than any other town in Great Britain. Probably the most valuable single source is the wonderful series of Letter Books, extracts from the first nine of which were published (1868) by the Corporation under the title *Memorials of London and London Life in the 13th, 14th, and 15th Centuries*, edited by H. T. Riley. *Calendars of Letter Books A–L, 1275–1498* were published (1899–1912) by the Corporation with R. R. Sharpe as editor. The Letter Books are so called because they are severally distinguished by a letter of the alphabet, and they contain the main, if not the only, existing record of the proceedings of the Court of Aldermen and the Court of Common Council before the fifteenth century. From 1416 the Corporation kept a Journal which, until 1495, records the proceedings of both the Court of Aldermen and the Court of Common Council; after 1495 the Court of Aldermen had its own record. The fifteenth-century volumes of the Journal, as yet unpublished, may, with caution, be used to illuminate the history of fourteenth-century London.

Another series of administrative records useful for this theme is the records of Bridge House. One can get some idea of the bequests to, and purchases of property for, the upkeep of London Bridge from the numerous deeds dating from the end of the twelfth century and from the rentals, which include receipts from fishmongers and butchers in Stocks Market, tolls for passage over and under the bridge, legacies, alms, and earnest money. The expenditure is chiefly on materials and wages of masons, carpenters, laborers, sailors, tidesmen, chaplains, and others. Even more interesting are the account rolls which start in 1381 and which typically begin with receipts from arrears, rents and farms, quit rents, tolls from the bridge, etc., and continue with debits for vacancies, rents payable by the bridge, salaries, and other expenses. These entries are followed by weekly paragraphs for receipts and expenses, including wages, expenses for maintenance and purchases, costs of feasts and ceremonies, etc. An abstract of the first account of 1381–82 is printed on pp. 256–57 of C. Welch's *History of the Tower Bridge* (1894). For the period 1350–70 two rolls of letters survive from the mayor, aldermen, and commonalty of the City of London, to provincial and foreign towns for repayment of tolls, surrender of apprentices, payment of debts, and many other commercial matters. They were edited by R. R.

Sharpe and published by the Corporation of London in 1885 as *Calendar of Letters from the Mayor and Corporation of the City of London, c. 1350–70.*

Of judicial records more series survive. The most generally useful are the Plea and Memoranda Rolls, which begin in 1323 and for which six volumes of calendars, covering the period 1323–1482 and edited by A. H. Thomas and P. E. Jones, have been published by the Corporation (1926–61). To some extent the early rolls are similar in character to the older Letter Books, but as time went on, the Letter Books increasingly confined themselves to the executive and administrative activities of the city authorities while the Rolls became increasingly legal in character. They tended to record especially pleas arising from public prosecutions, or entailing a fine to the king in addition to damages to the plaintiffs, the kind of case which was later to be heard in the London Quarter Sessions of the Peace. But in Chaucer's day the Rolls were still recording a wider range of legal business, including supervision of administration of estates of deceased persons, especially where the heirs were orphans and therefore wards of the city. Such supervision sometimes involved the production of a detailed inventory of the furniture and goods of the deceased, most valuable to historians.

Not much else of relevance has been published of the judicial records. For the Mayor's Court the only surviving records, apart from a few fragments for 1377, are the nine rolls from 1298 to 1307, for which A. H. Thomas edited a *Calendar of Early Mayor's Court Rolls, 1298–*

1307 for the City in 1924. The Mayor's Court had origi-
nally been closely connected with the Husting Court, but
by Chaucer's time the Mayor's Court was dealing more
with personal actions by plaint, leaving to the Husting
pleas by writ relating to lands and rents. The Husting
was the court where Londoners could prove wills, that
could bequeath land as well as chattels, and these hundreds of wills are a mine of information about the social
life of the time. From 1258 to 1688 they were calendared
by R. R. Sharpe and published by the Corporation (1889)
in two volumes entitled *Calendar of Wills Proved and
Enrolled in the Court of Husting, London, A.D. 1258–
1688*. The rest of the Husting Court Rolls remain in
manuscript at the Record Office, as do the surviving
Sheriffs' Court Rolls.

Of the royal judicial records of this period, the most
generally valuable are the nine coroners' rolls, 1300–
1301, 1321–40, 1367–68, calendared by R. R. Sharpe
and published by the Corporation in 1913. Helena Chew
has calendared the Escheat Rolls for 1340–77 and 1388–
89, and the Assizes of Novel Dissesin and Mort d'Ancestor held before the Coroner and Sheriffs between 1340
and 1436. The latter calendar was published in 1965 by
the London Record Society as *London Possessory Assizes:
A Calendar*. Financial records that throw light on the
social structure of London in the early fourteenth century
are *Two Early London Subsidy Rolls*, edited by E.
Ekwall (1951).

By the fourteenth and fifteenth centuries the city's self-
government was sufficiently established for some of its

officials to feel moved to write custumals. In 1311, Andrew Horn, city chamberlain, caused a book to be made which included charters and other customs of the city. Later in the reign of Edward II part of this was copied into a Liber Memorandorum, to which were added further statutes and customs in the reign of Edward III. Then later in the fourteenth century there was formed a Liber Custumarum of city customs, laws and charters, proceedings at royal judicial visits, and municipal regulations of the greatest variety. Part of this volume later became detached and is now Cottonian MS Claudius D 11 in the British Museum. Together these manuscripts consist of parts of two larger books, one of which was compiled before 1324 and the other later in the century. Some of this material found its way into the great Liber Albus, compiled by or for John Carpenter, common clerk or town clerk of the city and completed by November, 1419. The manuscript reflects London life in all its varied aspects during the fourteenth century and deals with customs, laws, social conditions, trade, and general conduct of the city government. The Liber Albus, together with the Liber Custumarum and parts of the Liber Memorandorum were edited by H. T. Riley and published in the Rolls Series in four volumes, 1859–62, under the title *Munimenta Gildhallae Londoniensis.*

By the time that the Liber Albus was compiled, the city not only had an archive of which it was proud, but a library soon to be enriched by the generosity of Richard Whittington. From that day to this London has had a fine Guildhall Library which, from 1863, began to be a repository of records arising within the city other than those of the Corporation itself. The Guildhall Library has now become a great archive of records such as deeds (about five thousand), ward, parish, and business records, and the muniments of city companies. For an excellent introduction to both city and guild records, see *A Guide to the Records in the Record Office and the Library Muniment Room*, by P. E. Jones and R. Smith (1951). Except for the guild archives, most of these records do not go back as far as the fourteenth or fifteenth centuries.

Even in the parochial records only a few churches have churchwardens' accounts for this period. The accounts of All Hallows, London Wall, from 1455–1536 were privately printed by Charles Welch in 1912; those for St. Mary-at-Hill, 1422–1559, were edited by H. Littlehales for the Early English Text Society, Original Series, Vols. 25 and 28, 1904–1905; those for St. Michael Cornhill, 1455 to 1608, were edited by W. H. Overall in 1869.

By contrast the records of city guilds are more plentiful for this period, even if for some it is only the charters that survive. The wealthiest city companies, like the Goldsmiths and the Mercers, have retained custody of their records, often now in the care of a trained librarian or archivist; most of the others have deposited their records in the Guildhall Library. Most of the major city companies have by now commissioned editions of their records, or of the history of the company, or both. Of these works the following are the most useful for this period; they are arranged alphabetically by guilds or companies, not by authors.

A. Pearce: *The History of the Butchers Company* (1929).

B. W. F. Alford and T. C. Barker: *A History of the Carpenters' Company* (1968).

Bower Marsh: *Records of the Carpenters' Company*, Vol. II (1914), Wardens Accounts, 1438–1516.

F. T. Phillips: *A Second History of the Worshipful Company of Cooks of London* (1966).

Historical Memoranda of the Coopers' Company, 1396–1848 (1848).

C. Welch: *History of the Cutlers of London*, 2 vols. (1923).

A. H. Johnson: *The History of the Worshipful Company of the Drapers of London*, especially Vol. I (1914).

T. Girtin: *The Triple Crowns: A Narrative History of the Drapers' Company, 1364–1964* (1964).

Drapers Company: Transcript of the Earliest Records (1910).

W. Herbert: *History of the Worshipful Company of Fishmongers* (1837).

T. C. Barker: *The Girdlers Company* (1957).

C. H. Ashdown: *History of the Glaziers Company, 1328–1918* (1919).

J. A. Kingdon: *Facsimile of the First Volume of MS Archives of the Worshipful Company of Grocers of the City of London, 1345–1463*, 2 vols. (1886).

J. A. Rees: *The Worshipful Company of Grocers* (1923).

L. Lyell and F. D. Witney: *Acts of Court of the Mercers Company* (C.U.P., 1936).

J. Watney: *An Account of the Mercers Company* (1914).

J. Watney: *Some Account of the Hospital of St. Thomas*

of Acon and the Plate of the Mercers Company (1892). In the fourteenth century the Mercers became the patrons of the hospital.

C. M. Clode: *The Early History of the Guild of Merchant Taylors* (1888).

H. L. Hopkinson: *Ancient Manuscript Books of the Merchant Taylors Company* (1915).

The Lord Mayors Pageants of the Merchant Taylors Company (1931).

J. Christie: *Some Account of the Parish Clerks* (1893).

C. Welch: *History of the Worshipful Company of Pewterers*, 2 vols. (1902).

P. E. Jones: *The Worshipful Company of Poulters* (2nd edn., 1965).

J. Steven Watson: *A History of the Salters Company* (1963).

E. M. Veale: *The English Fur Trade in the Later Middle Ages* (1966). Deals well with the Skinners Company.

J.J. Lambert: *Records of the Skinners of London* (1933).

A. C. Stanley Stone: *The Worshipful Company of Turners of London* (1925).

R. Champness: *The Worshipful Company of Turners of London* (1966).

T. Milbourn: *The Vintners Company* (London, 1888).

A. L. Simon: *The History of the Wine Trade in England*, 3 vols. (1906, reprinted 1964). Deals with the Vintners Company in the context of the wine trade.

Two valuable general works on the guilds are:

Herbert, W.: *The History of the Twelve Great Livery Companies*, 2 vols. (1836–37).

Unwin, G.: *The Gilds and Companies of London* (1908).

On the churches of medieval London, the following are useful:

Clarke, B. F. L.: *The Parish Churches of London* (1966).

Cobb, G.: *The Old Churches of London* (1961).

Cook, G. H.: *Old St. Paul's Cathedral* (1955).

Carpenter, E.: *A House of Kings: The History of Westminster Abbey* (1966).

Matthews, W. R., and Atkins, W. M., eds.: *A History of St. Paul's Cathedral* (1957). Chapter I, "Earliest Times to 1485," by C. N. L. Brooke.

Walters, H. B.: *London Churches at the Reformation* (1939).

Westlake, H. F.: *The Abbey of Westminster* (1920).

For the Inns of Court and other institutions of London, see:

Baildon, W. P.: *The Site of Lincoln's Inn* (1902).

Douthwaite, W. R.: *Gray's Inn* (1886).

Hay-Edwards, C. M.: *A History of Clifford's Inn* (1912).

Hope, W. H. St. John: *The History of the London Charterhouse* (1925).

Imray, J.: *The Charity of Richard Whittington* (1968).

Knowles, M. D., and Grimes, W. F.: *Charterhouse* (1954).

Odgers, W. B., ed.: *The Inns of Court and of Chancery* (1912).

Somerville, R.: *The Savoy, Manor, Hospital, Chapel* (1960).

Williamson, J. B.: *The History of the Temple* (2nd edn., 1925).

Williams, E.: *Staple Inn* (1906).

For maps of London for this period, see M. Honeybourne, *A Sketch Map of London under Richard II* (Publication No. 93, London Topographical Society, 1960), together with Miss Honeybourne's commentary on the map in the *London Topographical Record*, Vol. XXII (1965), "The Reconstructed Map of London under Richard II." See also the map of "The City of London in the Fifteenth Century" in C. L. Kingsford, *Prejudice and Promise in 15th Century England* (1925, reprinted 1962). For further topographical information, consult the articles in the *London Topographical Record*, especially those by C. L. Kingsford on medieval London houses in Vols. X, XI, and XII (1916, 1917, 1920) and by M. Honeybourne on "Charing Cross Riverside" and "The Fleet and its neighbourhood in early and medieval times," Vols. XIX (1947) and XXI (1958).

The London County Council's great *Survey of London*, still in progress, deliberately does not deal with the City, but gives detailed treatment to the surrounding areas, of which for this period Vol. XVI, *Charing Cross*, Vol. XVIII, *The Strand*, and Vol. XXII, *Southwark*, are specially useful. The *Survey of London* by the Elizabethan antiquary John Stow has a special value since he records sights and traditions now lost, and the edition by C. L. Kingsford (2 vols., 1908) supplies valuable notes by a distinguished historian of London. For the street names E. Ekwall's *Street Names of the City of London* (1954) has the great advantage of being written by an experienced philologist. The *Transactions* of the London and Middlesex Archaeological Society are valuable not only for the topography of London but for all aspects of its history.

Other topographical works useful for this period are:

Clarke, C. T.: *Bermondsey, Its Historic Memories and Associations* (1902).

Home, G.: *Old London Bridge* (1931).

Hobhouse, H.: *The Ward of Cheap* (1959).

Johnson, D. J.: *Southwark and the City* (1969).

Knight, A. C.: *Cordwainer Ward* (1917).

Welch, C.: *History of the Tower Bridge and of Other Bridges over the Thames* (1894). The first 127 pages deal with Old London Bridge.

Westlake, H. F.: *Westminster* (1919).

White, J. G.: *History of the Ward of Walbrook* (1904).

Other works useful for this subject are:

Baker, Timothy: *Medieval London* (1970).

Beardwood, A.: *Alien Merchants in England, 1350–77* (1931).

Selected Bibliography

Benham, W., and Welch, C.: *Medieval London* (1911).

Besant, W.: *Medieval London,* 2 vols. (1906).

Bird, R.: *The Turbulent London of Richard II* (1949). A work of scholarship concerned primarily with the political struggles of the city in this period.

Brewer, D.: *Chaucer in his Time* (1963).

Carus-Wilson, E. M.: *Medieval Merchant Venturers; Collected Studies* (1954).

Crow, M. M., and Olson, C. C.: *Chaucer Life Records* (1966).

The Corporation of London, Its Origin, Constitution, Powers and Duties (1950). An official publication concerned primarily with the present position, but full of historical background.

Ekwall, E.: *Studies on the Population of Medieval London* (1956).

Hollaender, A. E. J., and Kellaway, W.: *Studies in London History presented to Philip E. Jones* (1969). This scholarly volume by well-established historians of London contains nine essays that are of relevance for this period.

McKisack, M.: "London and the Succession to the Crown during the Middle Ages" in *Studies in Medieval History presented to F. M. Powicke* (1948).

Pendrill, C.: *London Life in the 14th Century* (1925).

Robertson, D. W.: *Chaucer's London* (1968).

Sharpe, R. R.: *London and the Kingdom,* 3 vols. (1894–95).

Thomas, A. H.: "Life in Medieval London," in *Journal*

of *the British Archaeological Association*, New Series, Vol. 35 (1929–30).

Thrupp, S.: *The Merchant Class of Medieval London* (1948) is a work of scholarship which has a wealth of references to sources.

Tout, T. F.: "The Beginnings of a Modern Capital," in *Collected Papers*, Vol. 3, Manchester University Historical Series, 66 (1934).

Williams, G. A.: *Medieval London, from Commune to Capital* (1963). Concerned with the government of London in the twelfth and thirteenth centuries and thus forms a prelude to the period treated in this volume.

The main collections of objects from London for this period are those in the London Museum and the Guildhall Museum, at present kept respectively in Kensington Palace and premises in Bassishaw High Walk near the Guildhall. It is intended to amalgamate these collections when a new Museum of London has been built. There is no up-to-date catalog; the most useful one is the *Medieval Catalogue* of the British Museum, issued in 1940 and reprinted in 1967. Other objects relative to the history of London in this period will be found in the British Museum.

Of books dealing with surviving buildings perhaps the most useful are the two volumes on London in the *Buildings of England* series, edited by Sir Nikolaus Pevsner and published by Penguin Books. Volume I, which describes the cities of London and Westminster, was first published in 1957 and revised in 1962; Volume II, which covers the outer areas and therefore treats of suburbs like Clerkenwell, Spitalfields, Southwark, and Lambeth, was published in 1952 and is under revision. The Royal Commission on the Ancient and Historical Monuments of England has five volumes dealing with London: I, *Westminster Abbey*, II, *West London*, and IV, *The City* have material relevant to London in this period. *A History of the King's Works*, edited by H. M. Colvin (3 vols., 1963) is useful for the Tower of London and Westminster Hall.

Addendum

Recently there have appeared three articles that are useful for this subject:

Barron, Caroline M.: "The Quarrel of Richard II with London 1392–7," in *The Reign of Richard II: Essays in Honour of May McKisack*, ed. F. R. H. Du Boulay and Caroline M. Barron (1971), pp. 173–201.

Brown, A. L.: "The Privy Seal Clerks in the Early 15th Century," in *The Study of Medieval Records, Essays in Honour of Kathleen Major*, ed. D. A. Bullough and R. L. Storey (1971), pp. 261–81.

Martin, G. H.: "The Registration of Deeds of Title in the Medieval Borough," in *The Study of Medieval Records, Essays in Honour of Kathleen Major*, ed. D. A. Bullough and R. L. Storey (1971), pp. 151–73.

Index

226

Index